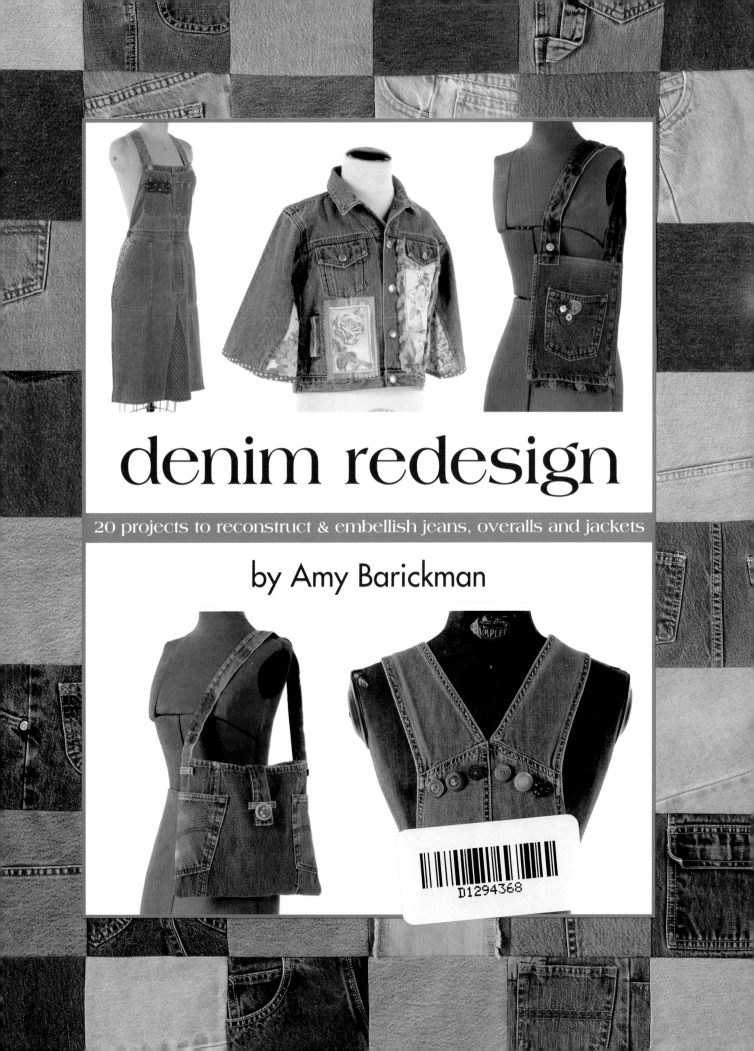

denim redesign

by Amy Barickman

D1294368

acknowledgments

My special thanks and appreciation go to all those who shared my vision for this title and created projects for this book: Mary Ann Donze, Donna Martin, Diane McCauley, Secely Palmer and Diane Sudhoff. A particular thanks goes to Mary Ann Donze for sharing her one-of–a-kind design style, careful illustrations and editorial content; to Secely Palmer for her dedication and enthusiasm throughout the entire process from concept to design and editing; to Kayte Price for her cover design and photo styling; to Tracy Thompson for her photography; to Desiree Mueller for styling the book and her attention to detail in the production and layout of the text. And, I am also grateful to Nancy Zieman and her team, who encouraged me to pursue this content for presentation in a two-part series on PBS's *Sewing with Nancy*.

DESIGNER CREDITS

Mary Ann Donze
The Hipster Skirt
Revered Remnant Skirt
Denim Montage Skirt
Imagine Jeans
Vintage Rose Jacket
Flower Power with
  Ruffles Jacket
Pocket Collage
  Shoulder Bag

Secely Palmer
Whatever Life Sends
  You Apron
I'm Back Bib
  Overalls Apron
Be Still My Heart
  Utility Apron
My Way Jean Front Apron
Two-Pocket Purse
One-Pocket Yo-yo Bag
Laptop Tote

Donna Martin
Vintage Voyage Jeans
Yarn Swirl Jeans
Yarn Medley Jacket

Diane Sudcoff
Groovy Godets Skirt

Diane McCauley
Aztec Accent Jacket

Becky Larson
Denim Quest Quilt

about the author

Amy Barickman is a leader in the sewing and craft pattern design industry. After graduating from the University of Kansas with a degree in art and design, she founded Indygo Junction in 1990 to publish and market books and patterns designed by fresh, new talent. Amy's vision for anticipating popular trends has led her to discover artists and guide them to create with innovative materials and tools.

As technology improved she envisioned what crafters might accomplish with their home computer and printer. She founded The Vintage Workshop in 2002 to create products that combine timeless vintage artwork with the computer and inkjet printable materials using downloads from her website and CDs.

To date Amy has identified and marketed more than 25 designers and published 600 pattern titles and 70 books, including her recent releases **Indygo Junction's Needle Felting** and **The Vintage Workshop's Art-to-Wear**. She inspires countless crafters to open their own creative spirit and experiment with the newest sewing, fabric and crafting techniques.

Barickman's work has been featured in several magazines including a recent honor as one of *Country Living's* 2007 Women Entrepreneurs Celebration of Creativity. She has made television appearances on HGTV, *America Quilts*, and *Sewing with Nancy*.

©2007 Amy Barickman, Indygo Junction Inc.

Published by Indygo Junction
P.O. Box 30238 • Kansas City , MO 64112
913-341-5559 • www.indygojunction.com

ISBN-10 0-9754918-1-4
ISBN-13 978-0-9754918-1-2

We take great care to ensure that the information included in our patterns is accurate and presented in good faith. No warranty is provided nor results guaranteed. For your convenience, we post an up-to-date listing of corrections on our website www.indygojunction.com. If a correction is not noted, please contact our customer service department at info@ indygojunction.com or 913-341-5559. You may also write us at PO Box 30238, Kansas City, MO 64112.

history of denim fabric and jeans

Denim has been produced in this country since the late 18th century and is a twill woven fabric, most often made from cotton, and used for jeans, overalls, jackets, shirts, etc. Reference books say the origin of the word "denim" is an English version of the French word "serge de Nimes," a durable silk and wool twill fabric from the town of Nimes in France. Around the same time sailors from Genoa, Italy, wore uniforms made from cotton/linen/wool mix called "fustian" and it happened to be blue. The fabric became known as "jeans" from the sailors who wore it. It is important to note that although both denim and jean were relatively

coarse fabrics woven from a wool blend, denim consisted of one dark colored thread and one white thread. Jean, on the other hand, was woven from two threads of the same color. By the 18th century, denim and jean had arrived on the shores of the New World. While the long lasting cloth was prefect for the harsh conditions workers and settlers faced on a daily basis, it wasn't long until cotton crops prompted Americans to start manufacturing their own domestically produced 100% cotton denim and jean fabric colored blue using indigo dye. The Merriam-Webster dictionary added the word "denim" to its collection of definitions, describing it "as a coarse cotton drilling used for overalls, etc."

Denim has since become an American icon. Blue denim is truly miraculous—hard wearing, relatively cheap, comfortable, warm in winter, cool in summer and oddly neutral in color—almost everything seems to match it. Denim keeps its shape and hides the dirt until you throw it into the wash. Functional yet stylish, the more you wear it, the more stylish it becomes.

table of contents

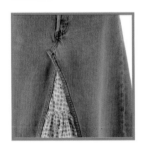

APRONS/UTILITY BELTS

PURSES/BAGS

MISCELLANEOUS

introduction

As a symbol of American culture, denim, is amazingly versatile. It can be repaired, altered, embroidered, and personalized. You can embellish and or stitch things on to it or rip it up. It is adaptable. You can make a statement without saying a word. Denim can make you distinctive. In fact by wearing denim, you can be whatever you want: feminine, youthful, a groupie, rustic, a leader or just plain hip!

This book introduces many different techniques for deconstructing and repurposing your denim wardrobe. We show you how to take ordinary well-worn denim jeans and overalls and make them into extraordinary one-of-a-kind skirts, purses, aprons, and quilts. Plain denim jackets are embellished with your favorite fabrics, heirloom embroidered linens, fibers and vintage images to create a new look for your old stand-bys. By using simple techniques easy enough for any level seamstress, you can redesign traditional denim pieces that you will enjoy in your everyday lifestyle.

Techniques described in this book include how to take a collage of assorted yarns and apply them to water-soluble stabilizer to construct new fiber fabrics and use them to embellish collars and cuffs of denim jackets. Vintage images are printed on to printable fabrics from your computer and an inkjet printer and then used to customize your denim wearables. The images mentioned in this book can be purchased and downloaded from www.thevintageworkshop.com.

Using vintage aprons and buttons, lush fabric remnants, recycled denim scraps, fibers, quilting cottons, vintage images and decorative stitching you can transform any ordinary denim garment into an amazing piece of wearable art!

IMAGE APPLIQUÉ AND COLLAGE

Several projects in this book have been embellished with images from The Vintage Workshop. Images can be printed directly to fabric that can then be stitched or fused in place or they can be printed to an iron-on transfer material that can then be ironed on. For both methods you can use your home computer and an inkjet printer.

If you prefer a no-sew process, iron-on transfers work well when you want an image applied to denim. However, images printed to fabrics allow more versatility. Most projects in this book use images printed to fabrics that are then stitched in place. Decorative stitching, beading, even iron-on rhinestones can be easily affixed to a printed fabric image. The art and additional embellishments make wonderful accents to denim surfaces. Create designer-style fashions for a fraction of the designer cost!

PRINTING IMAGES TO FABRIC AND TRANSFERS

Most projects use Printable Cotton Poplin, Linen, or Cotton Canvas fabric sheets from The Vintage Workshop. Fabric choice is a personal preference. We love the texture of the Linen and Canvas with denim. Poplin also works well and has a smooth finish that retains more detail than Linen and Canvas. But, mixing different printable fabrics in one project adds depth and interest to the finished look. We also recommend transfers from The Vintage Workshop—Iron-on Transfer I is translucent and Iron-on Transfer II is opaque. Experiment with different fabrics and transfers to find your favorites.

Here are some basic instructions for using printable fabrics and iron-ons. Remember to always read and follow the manufacturer's instructions for the best results.

PRINTING AN IMAGE ON FABRIC

To print an image you will need:

- An image from a CD or Download Collection or from any source
- Computer and inkjet printer
- Vintage Workshop fabric sheet
- Steam-a-Seam fusible web (optional)
- Iron
- Scissors

1. Print the image onto a fabric sheet following the instructions on the fabric packaging.

2. Use scissors to roughly cut out the image following the project instructions.

3. Remove paper backing from the fabric sheet.

4. Optional: Apply Steam-a-Seam fusible web to the back of the fabric image, following the manufacturer's instructions. Trim image as desired.

5. Remove paper backing from the fusible web. Place the image on the project fabric, right side up. Fuse in place. Add embellishments as desired.

Note: Images on fabric may also have the edges pressed under, pinned and stitched close to the fold or simply left raw and zigzagged.

MAKING AN IRON-ON TRANSFER

To print an iron-on transfer you will need:

- An image from a CD or Download Collection or from any source
- Computer and inkjet printer
- Iron-on Transfer I or II from The Vintage Workshop
- Iron
- Scissors

1. Print the image onto an iron-on transfer sheet, following the instructions on the packaging

2. Use the scissors to cut out the image on the outline.

3. Remove the paper backing. Place the image face-up on the project fabric. Lay the parchment pressing sheet on top. Press with a dry iron following manufacturer's instructions to complete the transfer.

GENERAL INSTRUCTIONS

The following information and abbreviations apply to most projects in this book, unless stated otherwise:

- Read all instructions thoroughly before beginning
- All seam allowances are ½", unless noted otherwise
- RST = Right Sides Together
- RSO = Right Side Out
- WST = Wrong Sides Together
- WSO = Wrong Side Out

STITCH ILLUSTRATIONS

RUNNING STITCH

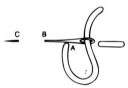

BLANKET STITCH

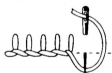

ALTERNATE CROTCH CLOSURE FOR DENIM SKIRTS

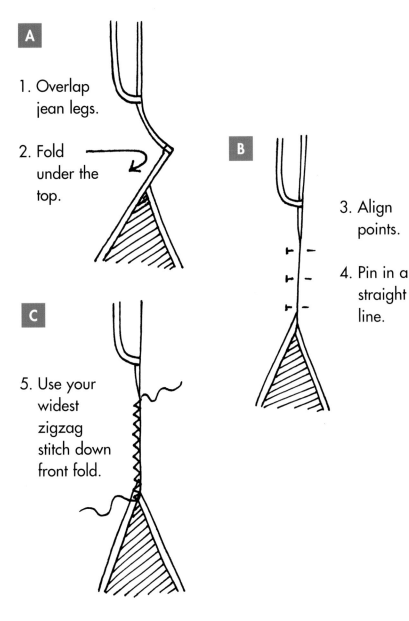

A

1. Overlap jean legs.

2. Fold under the top.

B

3. Align points.

4. Pin in a straight line.

C

5. Use your widest zigzag stitch down front fold.

D

6. Straight stitch next to zigzag visible on wrong side.

E

7. Remove zigzag stitch and trim away excess fabric.

FEATURED ARTWORK

Listed below are images used on the projects in this book along with their sources. Let our projects inspire your creativity. Seek out your own vintage ephemera to scan or copy to fabric, or visit www.thevintageworkshop.com to view a broad selection of download-able artwork for purchase. Any of the collections can be sent to you on a CD.

Imagine Jeans

- *Venus de Milo*, *The Connoisseur*, and *Dancers* from Download Collection **Fine Art I IE406**

- *Blond Maiden* from Download Collection **Fair Maidens IE410**

Vintage Rose Jacket

- *Baby in Tub* from CD **VW308 Little Ones**

- *Rose in Vase* and *Rose* from CD **VW307 Sweet Roses**

Flower Power w/ Ruffles Jacket

- *Rose*, *Rose with Cherub*, *Baby on Flowers*, and *Baby on Roses* from CD **VW308 Little Ones**

Pocket Collage

- *Ferris Wheel*, *Atlantic City*, *Map*, and *Riviera* from **The Vintage Workshop's Art-to-Wear** book with CD

- *Japanese Lantern* from Download Collection **IE410 Boys & Girls**

the hipster skirt

Three elements from the past combine to create this artsy skirt: one pair of well-worn jeans, one vintage apron and one vintage button. This skirt, with waistband removed, sits below the waist, fastened with a confident tab and button closure. Find a saucy vintage apron for the front inset or make a similar inset piece from new fabric. The lower edge is left unfinished to convey your fun and free spirited attitude.

DISASSEMBLY AND PREPARATION OF JEANS

1. With seam ripper, remove all belt loops. Set aside.

2. Cut off entire waistband just next to lower edge. Set aside. **SEE FIG. A.**

3. Beginning at the top of the side seam of the jeans with the waistband removed, measure down approximately 28⅜" on each side. Cut across both legs at this point. Set aside the lower leg sections. **SEE FIG. B.**

4. On each leg, cut just next to INNER double seam all the way to crotch seam, being certain to keep the double inner seam intact.

5. When you reach the crotch seam, cut just next to the double crotch seam, stopping about ¼" beneath the bottom point of zipper. **SEE FIG. C.**

MATERIALS NEEDED

- One pair of worn jeans that fit (the sample uses Levis 501 button front jeans)

- One vintage apron OR ⅔ yard fabric for front inset

- One vintage or new button approximately 1⅛". Use as large a button as possible that will fit through the buttonhole of your jean's waistband.

- Denim needle for machine, seam ripper, thread for use with denim

6. Turn jeans over. On the back cut just next to the double center crotch seam up about 5" or until you can create a fairly flat surface by lapping the left side over the right. **SEE FIG. D.**

7. On the back side, when you have it as flat as possible, pin along the overlapped edge. Remember that it may have slight puckers or pulls but this is fine as they will not be noticeable when worn. Stitch along the edge of the double back seam. **SEE FIG. E.**

8. On the front of the jeans, lap the right side over the left until flat. Pin and stitch around the edge of the double crotch seam. **SEE FIG. F.**

ASSEMBLY INSTRUCTIONS

1. Position all belt loops in approximately their original position but with their upper edge flush with upper raw edge of jeans. Pin. Stitch across upper and lower folded edges of belt loops.

2. Using the heavy thread for use with denim, do a zigzag stitch around the entire upper edge of the jeans, stitching over belt loops. If your jeans have rivets along the upper edge, stop stitching at these, backstitch and continue on the other side. **SEE FIG. G.**

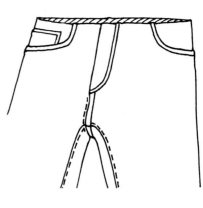

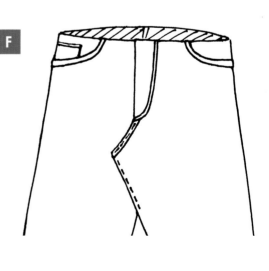
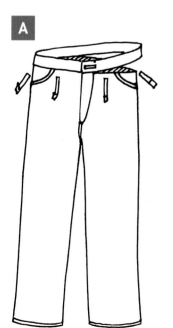
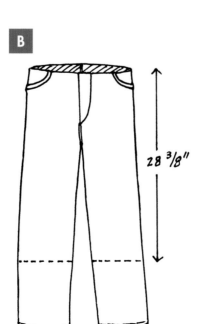

28 ³/₈"

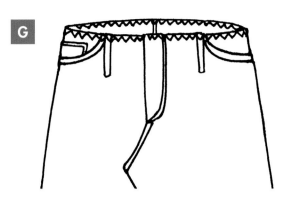

G

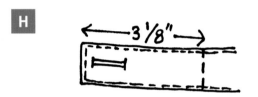

H

$3\frac{1}{8}"$

I

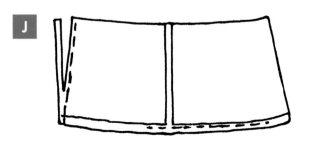

J

3. From the end of your waistband with the buttonhole, cut a section 3⅛" long to form tab. Pin the cut end of tab on the left side of the jeans about ½" beyond zipper stitching. The long upper edge of tab should be flush with upper edge of the jeans. Stitch along the cut end of tab to secure to jeans. Sew button on right side of jeans beneath buttonhole. **SEE FIGS. H & I.**

4. Deconstruct the previously cutoff lower leg sections as follows: on one leg cut along INNER double seam and open out the leg. Cut off the thick inner seam. **SEE FIG. J.**

With seam ripper, remove hem stitching from leg. Unfold the hem and press flat revealing the interesting gradations of color. Cut the remaining leg along the INNER double seam as well and open out. There is no need to remove hem.

5. From these lower leg sections you will construct the back skirt inset. Take measurements of the triangle shape left open on the back. It will vary with each jean. You will piece together the jeans leg fabric to fill this space, but be certain to allow extra fabric on the sides and upper point so that it can slide UNDER the jeans legs. The lower wide half of the triangle is composed of the first jeans leg with hem removed. Center the side seam of the jeans right side up, having the opened out hem serve as the bottom of the triangle. From the second leg, use the WRONG side of the fabric with side seam exposed to form the upper part of the triangle. Position the side seam so that it runs diagonally across the piece. Lap this upper section OVER the lower section. Pin and do a zigzag stitch across to connect them. **SEE FIG. K.**

6. On the back, with the right side up, slide the completed triangle UNDER the jeans legs. Pin all edges and stitch close to raw edge. On the inside, trim away any excess fabric of denim inset.

7. On the front, measure the triangular opening. Use this measurement to cut a triangle from the center front of your apron, allowing the hem of apron to serve as the wide lower edge of the triangle. Remember to cut extra fabric on sides and upper point to allow inset to slide under jeans legs. Finish raw edges of fabric triangular inset. **SEE. FIG. L.**

NOTE: If you do not have an apron for front inset, cut a triangle of fabric to match your measurement. Hem the lower edge, adding rickrack, etc. if desired. Finish the sides and upper point and apply as directed below.

8. With the right sides up, slide the apron inset UNDER the jeans legs. Pin all edges and stitch close to edge of jeans.

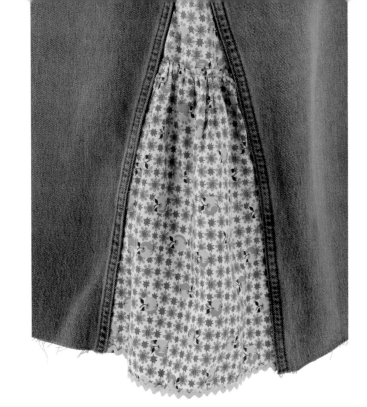

K

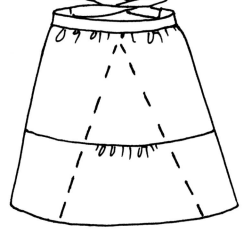

L

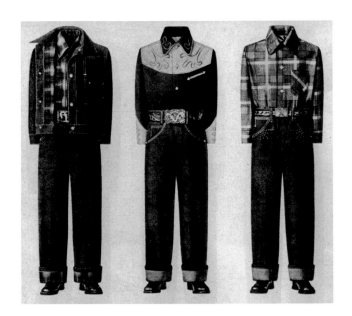

revered remnant skirt

Showcase a few of your treasured fabric remnants by piecing them together for this skirt's front and back insets. Use your imagination to combine rich velvets, vintage bark cloth and decorator fabrics. A whimsical belt cut from a jeans waistband spans the back inset where it is anchored with two opposing vintage buttons. An inside out hem hand stitched with embroidery floss does a quaint dance around the lower edge.

DISASSEMBLY AND PREPARATION OF JEANS

1. Beginning at top of waistband on each side of jeans, measure down 27¼". Cut across both legs at this point. Save lower leg sections for other projects! **SEE FIG. A.**

2. Follow steps 4 through 8 from **The Hipster Skirt** directions.

ASSEMBLY INSTRUCTIONS

1. Press lower edge to OUTSIDE ½" to form an inside out hem. With three strands of embroidery floss, do a running stitch around hem about ⅛" below upturned raw edge. **SEE. FIG. B.**

2. Construct the front and back insets as follows: with skirt lying flat, take measurements of the triangular openings on the front and back and record them. They will differ. Draw a triangle on a piece of paper (newspaper will do) the size of your triangle

MATERIALS NEEDED

- One pair of worn jeans that fit (the sample uses Levis 501 button front jeans)

- Waistband from an additional pair of jeans

- Two mismatched vintage or new buttons, approximately 1⅛"

- Four different fabric remnants for front and back insets

- One color embroidery floss and needle, thread for use with denim, denim needle for your machine

to use as a pattern. Add ½" to the lower edge to allow for a hem. Add an inch to sides and upper point so that finished inset can slide under the jeans legs. On each triangle cut across horizontally at some point to form an upper point section and a lower base section of the triangle. Label these pattern pieces "upper and lower front pieces" and "upper and lower back pieces." Use these patterns to cut from four different fabrics.

NOTE: When cutting fabric pieces, add ¼" to upper edge of the lower base section and add ¼" to the lower edge of the upper point section. This provides a seam allowance to connect them. For both the front and back fabric pieces, with right sides together, pin and stitch the two sections together in ¼" seam to form your triangular insets. **SEE FIG. C.**

Press seam allowance open. Along the lower edge of both triangles press to the wrong side a ¼", twice. Stitch to close hem. Finish sides and upper point of completed inset with serging or machine finishing stitch. **SEE FIG. D.**

3. With the right sides up, position completed front inset centered under leg fronts, aligning hemmed edge with lower edge of jeans legs. Pin around all edges. Stitch close to edge of jeans legs through the fabric beneath.

4. Position completed back inset in the same manner. Stitch in place. Use a zigzag stitch if desired.

5. Measure the width of your back inset across the connecting seam. Add 4" to this measurement and record. **SEE FIG. E.**

From your additional jeans waistband cut a length that is this final measurement to form the belt. On each end cut a slight diagonal as shown. **SEE FIG. F.**

Stitch a buttonhole close to each end of belt to fit your buttons. **SEE FIG. G.**

Place belt across connecting seam and mark position of buttons on skirt beneath. Stitch buttons on at this mark.

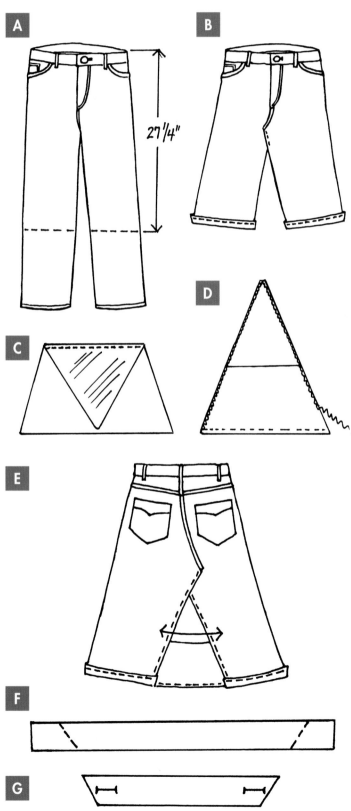

denim montage skirt

This is a longer length skirt created entirely from recycled denim with vintage button baubles, lace scraps and decorative stitching to add visual interest and texture. The long insets provide perfect palettes for playing with your denim scraps. Show wrong sides, right sides, seams and raw edges for a modern denim montage with handmade style.

DISASSEMBLY AND PREPARATION OF JEANS

1. Beginning at the top of the waistband, measure down approximately 33½" on each side. Cut across both legs at this point. From these cut off leg sections, remove INNER double seam from one lower leg and the SIDE single seam from the other lower leg. These can be used in construction of the insets. Set aside lower leg sections. **SEE FIG. A.**

2. Follow steps 4 through 7 from **The Hipster Skirt** directions.

3. Turn jeans WSO and align front sections of legs. With RST, pin in a straight line downward from bottom point of zipper for about 6", stopping at edge of jeans legs. Stitch straight down and backstitch to secure when you reach leg edge. Trim excess fabric, leaving a ½" seam allowance. Press open. **SEE FIG. B.**

MATERIALS NEEDED

- One pair of worn jeans that fit you

- A variety of denim pieces left over from previous projects OR an additional pair of old jeans (any size) to deconstruct to form the front and back insets

- Approx. 28 vintage or new buttons of various sizes. Sample uses natural shell and pearl vintage buttons.

- Two 6" to 10" lengths of vintage or tea stained natural colored lace. Sample uses vintage cotton crocheted lace.

- One color embroidery floss and needle

- Seam ripper, denim needle for your machine, thread for use with denim

4. Turn jeans RSO.

With seam ripper, remove hems from both lower leg sections that were cut off in Step 1; unfold both hems and press denim flat. You will use these sections to construct the front and back insets along with additional denim jean scraps.

ASSEMBLY INSTRUCTIONS

Construct the front and back insets as follows:

1. Take measurements of the triangular opening on the front and back and record them. They will differ. Draw a triangle on a piece of paper (newspaper will work) the size of your triangular opening to use as a pattern. Add 1" to each side and the upper point so that the finished inset can slide under the jeans legs. Cut out this completed pattern to use as a guide. When cutting sections to put together to equal the size of the skirt triangle, remember to allow extra fabric to overlap.

BACK INSET

The back inset of sample is comprised of three sections: an opened out hem section (right side), and two leg sections (wrong side) with side seam exposed. Instead of making traditional enclosed seams to connect these pieces, overlap them at least ¼", pin and stitch across with a variety of stitches. The raw edges add visual interest. See illustration to use as a guide. Finish the side edges and top point of your inset with serging, etc. Set aside. **SEE FIG. C.**

FRONT INSET

Similarly, the front inset is comprised of three sections: an opened out hem section (right side) on top, the wrong side of a leg section with side seam exposed in the center, and the right side of a lower leg section with hem unfolded and the inner seam running vertically through it on the bottom of triangle. Complete this section as follows:

A

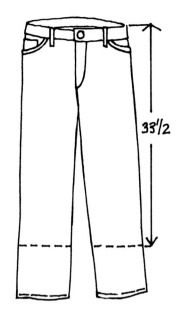

33½

B

C

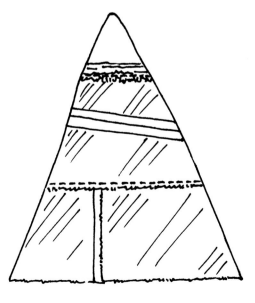

SKIRTS

17

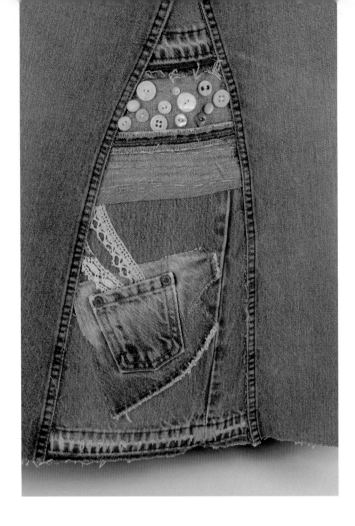

Instead of making traditional enclosed seams to connect these pieces, overlap them at least ¼", pin and stitch across with a variety of stitches. On top of this completed triangle is appliquéd an irregularly shaped section of jean discarded from another project. It is a piece that includes the small watch pocket found on many styles of jeans. It is placed at an angle and stitched to the inset with zigzag and straight stitches. Two pieces of vintage crocheted lace are placed in the pocket and stitched at a diagonal across the inset. The center section of inset has the lower edge turned up to the outside about ¾". It is pressed and then 3 strands of embroidery floss are used to do a running stitch across folded area and again 1½" above it. A variety of decorative stitches are applied horizontally to this inset. Thirteen vintage buttons of various sizes are randomly stitched to inset in a cluster. Finish the side edges and top point of your inset with serging, etc. **SEE FIG. D.**

2. Attach BOTH insets as follows: with right sides up, slide the completed inset under the jeans legs, centering them under the upper point and aligning the raw lower edges of inset with the lower edge of jeans. Pin inset to jean on the RIGHT side of garment, close to edge of the jeans leg. Using thread for use with denim, stitch inset to jeans to form skirt.

3. On the right pocket of jeans, stitch approximately 15 vintage or new buttons beneath curve of pocket. Refer to photograph for location and placement.

D

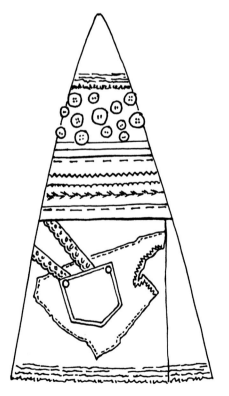

groovy godets skirt

This skirt is designed with a pleasing play of rugged denim and essentially feminine elements. The swingy fabrics, softly tied belt and jaunty kick of the godet skirt conceal its tough beginnings as a sturdy denim garment. Easily adapted to any size figure (including children), you need only begin with any denim skirt, shorts or jeans that fits you at the waist and upper hip. May be constructed in any length you desire following the directions provided. Experiment with a variety of quirky fabrics for belt and godets such as polyesters with a woven sparkle, decorator fabrics, or vintage linens.

MATERIALS NEEDED

■ **For the yoke:** Any pair of jeans, shorts, Capri's or skirt—any style will do EXCEPT pleated. The beauty of this pattern is all that has to fit is from waist to hip. It doesn't matter if the length isn't right or the silhouette is wrong or you spilled paint on the knees.

■ **For the denim panels:** An assortment of old jeans legs. Straight leg, boot cut and small flare legs all work well. Avoid bell-bottoms and extreme flares as well as tapered narrow legs.

You will need 2 complete legs (front and back hems are useable) for the side panels and enough useable hems for 4 front and back panels.

NOTE: if you are raiding your teen's closet for all that castoff denim, often the back hems have been walked on and abused. Unless you want that look, you will only get one panel out of the front of those legs.

■ **For the godets and belt:** Any lightweight fabric, woven or knit, will work and 2 D-rings. As pictured, 45" wide non-directional fabric, 6 of the largest godets and the belt requires ⅔ yard. If using one-way design or nap, 1 yard. Godet pattern pieces are provided.

Other suggestions for the godets and belt:

■ Try using up your coordinating quilt scraps. You will need six pieces 10" x 12"; piece together random pieces for the belt.

■ While mining in your teen's closet, gather up some old T-shirts for a variety of bright colored godets, or all versions of grey heather, or just classic white.

■ At the fabric store, purchase the same fabric in several colors, such as four pastel eyelets or two complementary polyesters with some woven sparkle.

FRONT TOO LOW

FRONT TOO HIGH

FRONT JUST RIGHT

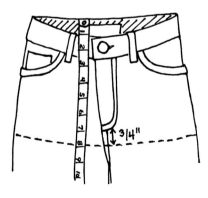

3/4"

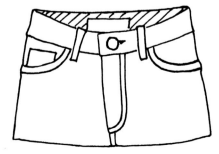

CUTTING INSTRUCTIONS FOR THE YOKE

1. Place your jeans on a table mimicking the natural curve of the waistband. If your jeans sit below your natural waistline, do not force the waistband to lie straight with the top of the front center and the top of the back waistband. **SEE FIGS. A, B, AND C.**

The length of the zipper fly will determine the length of the skirt yoke. Mark ¾" below all the thicknesses of the fly front. Measure from this mark to the top of the back waistband. Use this measurement to mark your jeans all the way around. **SEE FIG. D.**

NOTE: When marking the front, be sure to measure to the top of the back waistband.

So as not to cut off the bottom of your front pockets, fold and pin the inside of your front pockets well above your cutting line. Cut following this line.

HINT: Cut through both front and back at each side seam, then cut through just one layer all the way around. **SEE FIG. E.**

CUTTING INSTRUCTIONS FOR THE DENIM PANELS

Determine the length of the denim panels:

1. Try on your skirt yoke. It may ride higher without the legs pulling it down. Dangle a tape measure from the top of the waistband and record your desired finished length below:

Desired Finished Length:		_____"
Yoke Length, as cut:	−	_____"
Subtotal	=	_____"
Two ½" seam allowances	+	__1__"
Length to cut denim panels	=	_____"

Determine the width of your denim panels:

2. Measure all the way around the bottom edge of your cut yoke. Record this measurement below:

Yoke edge: _____ "

Number of panels (8): ÷ **8** "

Finished width of each panel: _____ "

Cut denim side panels:

3. Since most of us do not want, or need extra flare on our hips, the side seams use the flat felt seams of the jeans legs as the skirt side seam rather than godets.

a. Fold a jeans leg so the flat felt seam is on top and right next to the fold. Repeat, so you have one with the fold on the left side of the seam and one with the fold on the right side on the seam.

b. Measure from the finished hem up the fold and mark the desired cut length as determined in Step 1. (Point A)

c. At this mark, measure in from the fold and mark the desired panel width as determined in Step 2, PLUS a ½" seam allowance. (Point B)

d. At the hem, measure in from the fold the desired panel width PLUS a ½" seam allowance PLUS 1" for flare. (Point C)

e. Connect points A, B and C for your cutting lines. **SEE FIG. F.**

4. Cut both side panels. **SEE FIG. G.**

Cut front and back denim panels:

5. Lay each jean leg with the side seams aligned on top of each other. Generally, this will result in the fold lining up with the straight grain. Adjust as needed.

a. Measure from finished hem, up the leg and mark your desired cut length. (Point A)

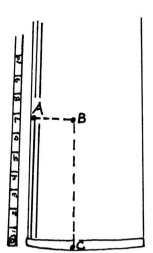

RIGHT OF FOLD   LEFT OF FOLD

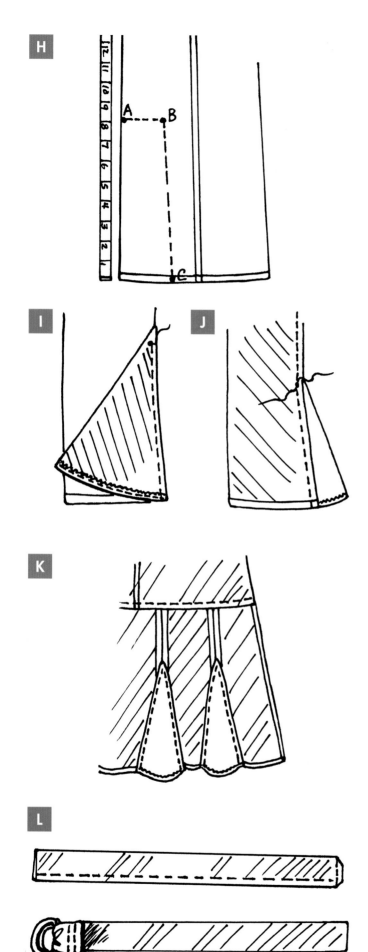

b. From Point A, measure and mark from the fold HALF the finished panel width PLUS a ½" for the seam allowance. (Point B)

c. At the hem, measure and mark from the fold HALF the desired panel width PLUS 1". This allows for a ½" seam allowance and a ½" for flare. (Point C)

d. Connect points A, B and C for your cutting lines. Cut out this panel and repeat for each panel, 3 more times. **SEE FIG. H.**

TIP: You can use this first panel as a pattern for the remaining panels.

CUTTING INSTRUCTIONS FOR THE GODETS

1. Reproduce the appropriate godet pattern piece provided for your skirt. See the OPTIONS note.

2. Cut six godets from your chosen fabric.

3. Finish and hem the bottom edges of your godets as desired.

ASSEMBLY INSTRUCTIONS

1. With right sides together, align the hem of a godet with the hem of a panel. Using a ½" seam allowance, stitch, stopping at the dot. Stitch the other side, again stopping at the dot. Continue with this method, connecting all denim panels and godets. **SEE FIG. I.**

CAUTION: Be sure to have the same number of denim panels between the side panels in both the front and the back.

2. With right sides together, stitch denim panels together from the top edge to the godet stitching. Continue with this method, connecting all the denim panels. **SEE FIG. J.**

HINT: Be sure to stop this stitching right before the godet stitching, being careful not to catch the godet in the stitching.

3. With the skirt portion complete and with RST, match the bottom raw edge of the yoke with the top raw edge of the skirt and the side seams, pin in place. Baste, easing these two skirt portions together, making any necessary adjustments to the panel seams to assure a smooth attachment to the yoke.

HINT: The side panel flat felt seams should line up just behind the side seams of the yoke. Serge, or finish the raw edges of the panel and godet seams.

4. Once all the adjustments have been made, stitch the skirt onto the yoke. Finish this seam with a zigzag stitch, etc. **SEE FIG. K.**

5. Press the yoke edge down. Press the godet and panel seams one of two ways. To maximize the godets, press the seam toward the godet. To minimize the godets, press the seam toward the denim.

ASSEMBLY INSTRUCTIONS FOR THE BELT

For your D-ring belt, fold a piece of fabric lengthwise (with right sides together) that is 5" wide by your waistband circumference, plus 12". Stitch a ½" seam allowance down the full length. Stitch one end at a right angle. Trim corners. Turn and press. Fold raw edge over about ½" and then fold through the flat side of two D-rings. Stitch securely, using two stitching rows. **SEE FIG. L.**

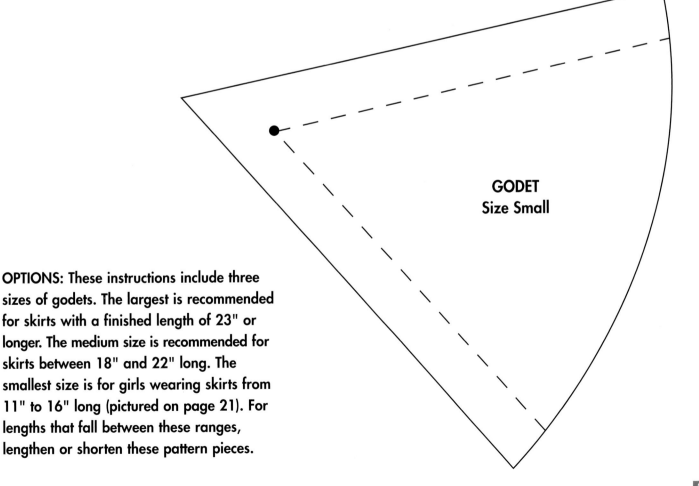

GODET
Size Small

OPTIONS: These instructions include three sizes of godets. The largest is recommended for skirts with a finished length of 23" or longer. The medium size is recommended for skirts between 18" and 22" long. The smallest size is for girls wearing skirts from 11" to 16" long (pictured on page 21). For lengths that fall between these ranges, lengthen or shorten these pattern pieces.

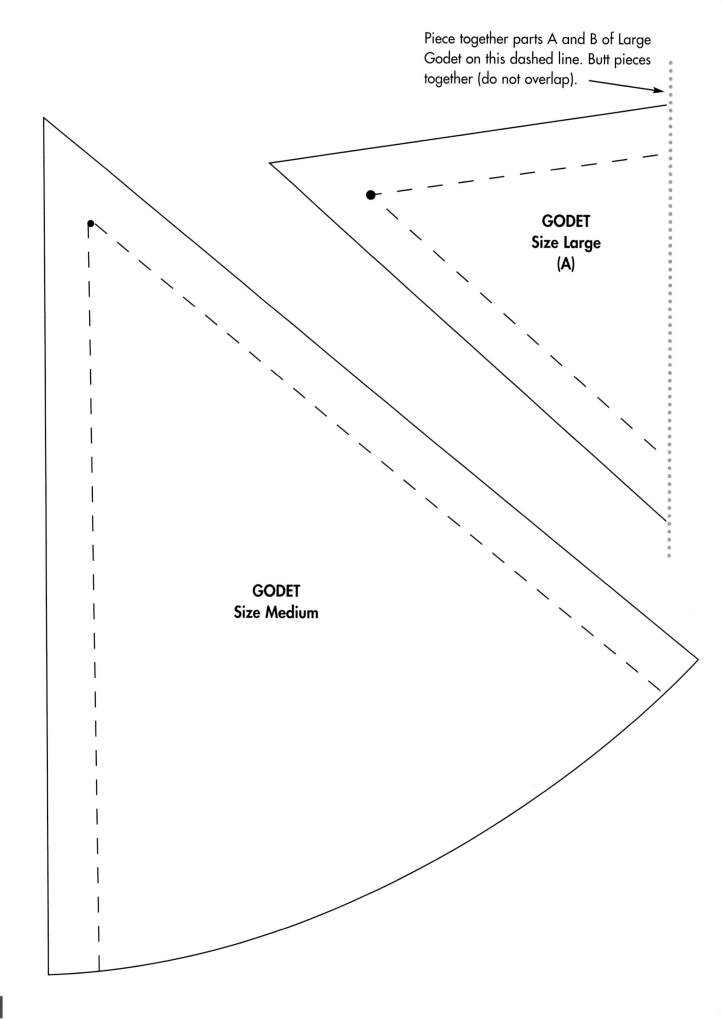

Piece together parts A and B of Large Godet on this dashed line. Butt pieces together (do not overlap).

GODET
Size Large
(A)

GODET
Size Medium

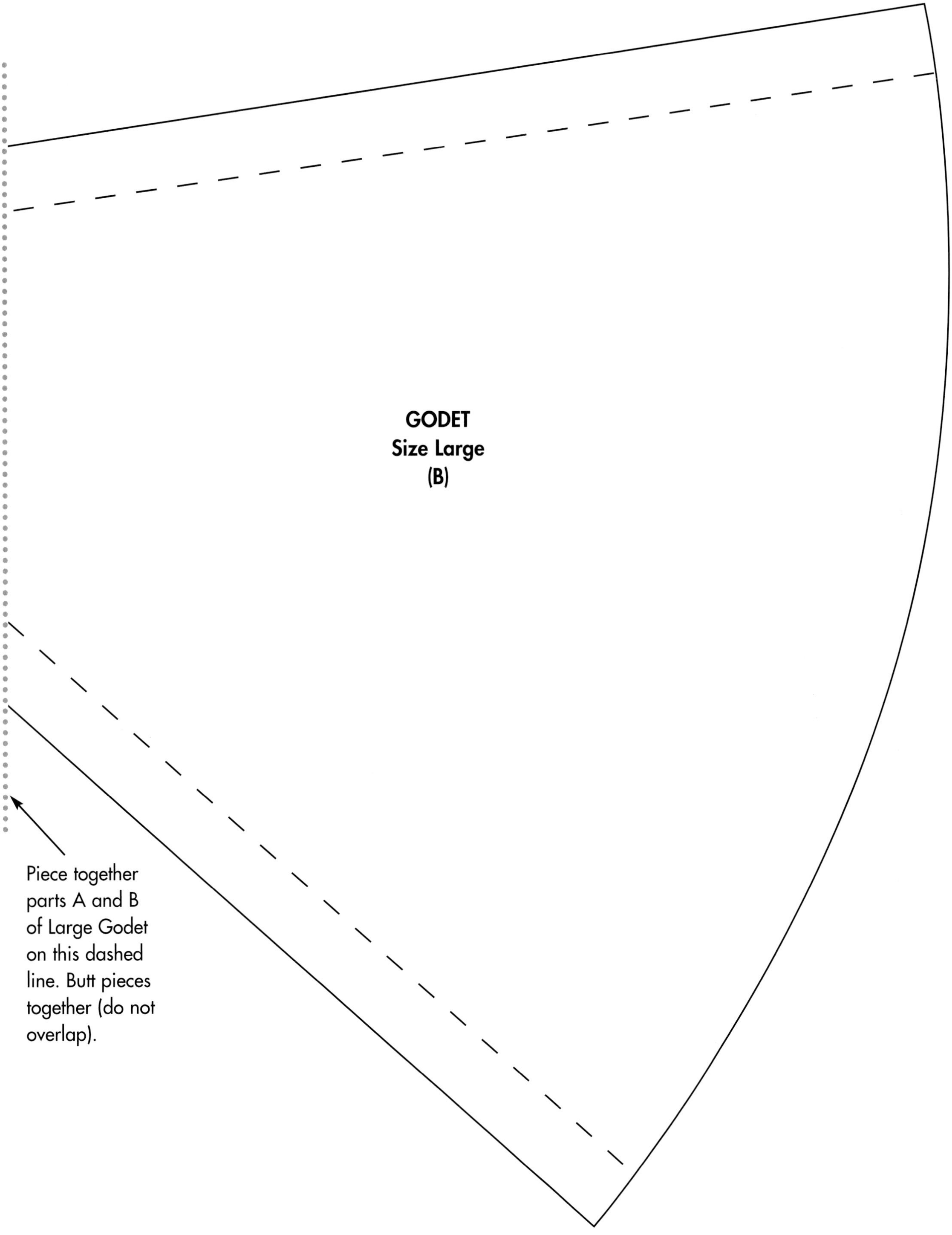

GODET
Size Large
(B)

Piece together
parts A and B
of Large Godet
on this dashed
line. Butt pieces
together (do not
overlap).

vintage voyage jeans

One pair of well-loved jeans combined with two fabrics in soft, time-worn hues create a jean of unique character. Add a smattering of whimsical fabric yo-yos, a length of fabric belt tied loosely at the waist and a fabric covered back pocket—and a new jean emerges to take you anywhere you travel.

MATERIALS NEEDED

- One pair of women's denim jeans that fit
- ⅓ yard of fabric for cuffs, belt, yo-yos and miscellaneous trim
- ⅓ yard of coordinating fabric for cuffs, belt, yo-yos and misc. trim
- 12" square of lightweight fusible interfacing
- Small Yo-Yo Maker by Clover Needlecraft *(If not using the Clover Yo-Yo Maker, instructions on how to make yo-yos are provided in the **Yarn Swirl Jeans** project.)*
- Thread (to coordinate with both fabrics)
- Denim needle for machine and thread for use with denim
- ***Optional:*** Chalk marker

CUTTING INSTRUCTIONS

1. From first fabric, cut two 2½" x 33" long strips for the belt and cut six 6½" high x 4½" wide rectangles for the cuffs. You may need more or less rectangles depending on the circumference of the leg at the bottom of the hem of the jeans you are using. Set aside.

2. From coordinating fabric, cut two 2½" x 33" long strips for the belt and cut six 6½" high x 4½" wide rectangles for the cuffs. You may need more or less rectangles depending on the circumference of the leg at the bottom of the hem of the jeans you are using. Set aside.

ASSEMBLY INSTRUCTIONS

1. Take one each of the two coordinating fabric cuff pieces and with RST stitch the long edges (6½" edges) together. Repeat this pattern until you have a total of six (three of each fabric) rectangles sewn together. Fabrics should alternate. Repeat this step with the other six rectangles. **SEE FIG. A.**

2. Press all the seams open on both of the assembled cuff strips.

3. Press to the wrong side a ½" hem on both long edges of the cuff strip. Repeat for second cuff strip. **SEE FIG. B.**

4. With WST, fold the cuff strip in half lengthwise, matching the two folded edges and press. Repeat for second cuff strip. **SEE FIG. C.**

5. Encase the bottom hemmed leg edge of the jeans inside the folded cuff strip. Make sure the bottom hem of your jeans is tight to the inside fold and that one short raw edge overlaps the inner leg seam by approximately ½". Wrap the cuff around the bottom of the jeans to the inner seam again. At this inner seam, fold the opposite short raw edge to the wrong side aligning with the inner seam. If there is an excessive amount of fabric to fold under, trim to a reasonable length. Pin all edges in place. Either machine stitch through all layers around the top folded edge of the cuff OR hand stitch both the exterior and the interior top folded edge of the cuff. Don't forget to stitch the inner seam of the cuff closed. Repeat for the second cuff strip. **SEE FIGS. D & E.**

6. Using the left back pocket as a pattern lay one of the coordinating fabrics wrong side up over the pocket and trace the outline of the pocket. Add a ½" seam allowance to this traced line and cut the pocket cover out. **SEE FIGS. F & G.**

7. Using the fabric pocket cover as a pattern piece, cut an interfacing piece and fuse to the wrong side of the fabric pocket cover piece.

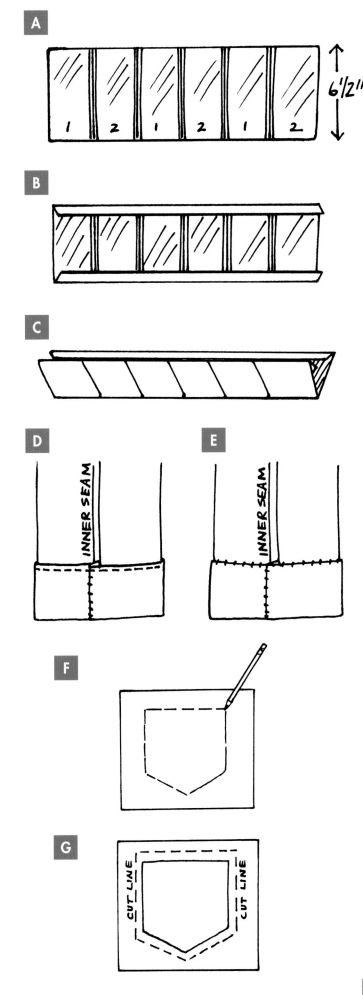

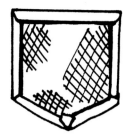

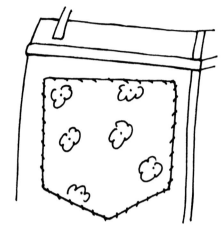

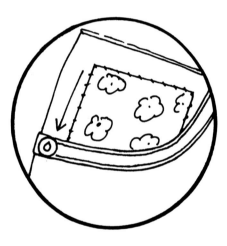

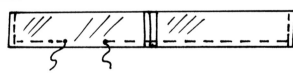

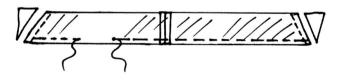

8. Press a ½" hem to the wrong side of the fabric pocket cover on all sides. **SEE FIG. H.**

9. Place and pin the fabric pocket cover onto the left jean pocket, making sure to align all the edges with each other. Hand stitch in place, hiding your stitches. **SEE FIG. I.**

10. Repeat Steps 6 through 9, for the right front inner pocket cover. Place as much of the fabric down into the front pocket as possible. Set aside. **SEE FIG. J.**

11. With your scraps from both the coordinating fabrics and using the small Clover Yo-Yo Maker, make four yo-yos from one fabric and make three yo-yos from the coordinating fabric. If you are not using the Clover Yo-Yo Maker refer to the instructions on *How to Make Yo-Yos* located in the **Yarn Swirl Jeans** project.

12. Pin and hand stitch three yo-yos in a cluster onto the top left-hand corner of the back fabric pocket cover. Be creative!

13. Pin and hand stitch three more yo-yos in a cluster to the top fabric cuff of one of the jeans legs. Refer to photograph. Stitch the final yo-yo to the opposite leg fabric cuff. Be even more creative! Set aside.

14. Take one each of the two coordinating fabric belt pieces and with RST stitch the short ends together. Repeat for the other two fabric belt pieces.

15. With RST and opposing fabrics of the two sewn belt strips lying on top of each other, stitch the two long edges of the belt. Leave an approximately 4" opening to turn. **SEE FIG. K.**

16. Stitch the two short ends of the belt together. If desired, you may stitch them on a diagonal and trim excess seam allowance. Turn belt right side out through opening and press. Slipstitch opening closed. **SEE FIG. L.**

17. Weave the finished belt through the belt loops and tie at the front.

28

yarn swirl jeans

An artfully redesigned jean has fabric insets at hem and needle felted swirls of yarn meandering here and there. Bouquets of charming fabric yo-yos centered with vintage buttons are scattered about. Choose muted, natural colors as shown or go with a more vibrant color palette. Amusing to wear, they are also great fun to create.

MATERIALS NEEDED

- One pair of women's denim jeans, any size
- Five fat quarters of different coordinating cotton fabrics
- Three yards of yarn
- 14 assorted coordinating buttons
- Small Yo-Yo Maker by Clover Needlecraft (*If not using the Clover Yo-Yo Maker, instructions on how to make yo-yos are provided.*)
- Thread (to coordinate with fabrics)
- Denim needle for machine, seam ripper, thread for use with denim
- Clover felting needle tool and mat
- *Optional:* Chalk marker

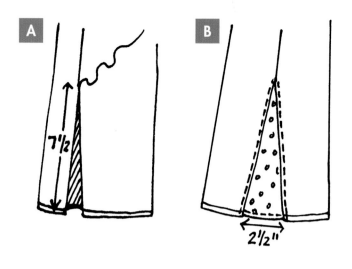

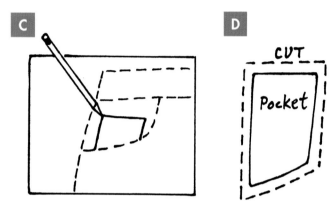

DISASSEMBLY OF JEANS

1. Using the seam ripper and starting at the hem, remove approximately 7½" of the side seams of both legs of your jeans. **SEE FIG. A.**

CUTTING INSTRUCTIONS

1. From one of the fabrics cut two rectangle pieces approximately 9" high by 4" wide.

ASSEMBLY INSTRUCTIONS

1. Hem one short edge of the fabric rectangles, using a ½" seam allowance.

2. With the right sides up, slide the fabric rectangle under the jeans side seam that was removed previously, centering and lining up the bottom hem of the fabric and the leg of the jeans. Spread the bottom hem of the jeans apart 2½", and pin. Top stitch the fabric in place. Trim the excess fabric from the wrong side. Repeat on the opposite leg. **SEE FIG. B.**

3. Using the right front inner pocket as a pattern, lay one of the coordinating fabrics right side up over the inner pocket and trace the outline of the pocket. Try to get as much of the fabric down into the pocket as possible. Add a ½" seam allowance to this traced line and cut the pocket cover out. **SEE FIGS. C & D.**

4. Using the fabric pocket cover as a pattern piece, cut an interfacing piece and fuse to the wrong side of the fabric pocket cover piece.

5. Press a ½" hem to the wrong side of the fabric pocket cover on all sides.

6. Place and pin the fabric pocket cover onto the right inner pocket, making sure to align all the edges with each other. Place as much of the fabric down into the front pocket as possible. Hand stitch in place, hiding your stitches. **SEE FIGS. E & F.**

NEEDLE FELTING INSTRUCTIONS

1. Place the felting needle mat inside the leg and/or the pocket of the jeans at the location where your yarn design will be placed. Refer to the photographs for the locations and the designs. Swirl the yarn onto the denim and tack into place with the felting needle tool until you have achieved the design you want. Needle felt the yarn into place. Couch over yarn for additional stability. Set aside.

HOW TO MAKE YO-YOS
without using the Clover Yo-Yo Maker

1. For 1¾" diameter yo-yos, cut out eleven 4" diameter fabric circles from your scraps of assorted coordinating fabrics. **FYI:** The cut fabric circles are twice the diameter of the desired finished yo-yo size plus a ½" for the seam allowance.

2. Finger press the raw edge of the circle a ¼" to the wrong side of the fabric, as you hand sew a running stitch close to the folded edge through both thicknesses. Use strong thread (knotted) and make sure it's long enough to go around the full circumference of the circle with some to spare. **SEE FIG. G.**

NOTE: Shorter stitches create a larger, more open center on your finished yo-yo. Longer stitches make a tighter finished yo-yo center. For this project the longer stitches are preferable. The tighter finished yo-yos look better.

3. Once you have stitched around the entire perimeter of the fabric circle, gently pull your stitching thread until the edges gather to the center. Make a couple of stitches to secure your gathers, then knot and trim your thread. Flatten your yo-yo with the gathers centered on the top of the yo-yo. **SEE FIG. H.**

EMBELLISHMENT INSTRUCTIONS

1. Refer to the photographs for suggested locations for the yo-yo and button placements. Pin and stitch the yo-yos with or without the buttons on top.

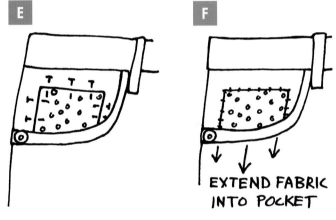

E

F

EXTEND FABRIC INTO POCKET

G

4" diameter circle

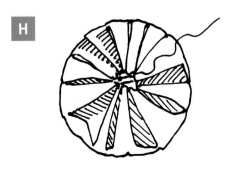

H

imagine jeans

Vintage images and lush fabrics get acquainted when they band together to create a unique embellishment adorning your jeans. Piece together scraps of your favorite medium-weight or decorator fabrics, interspersed with a touch of vintage textiles and buttons as well. Serging or other decorative stitching around fabric blocks add dimension. Overlay your diverse images, some of which have been cropped, tilted or tucked behind fabric to add an air of mystery. One back pocket has a "frame" cut out to hold a vintage image. A smattering of beads at the corner catches the eye.

MATERIALS NEEDED

- One pair of jeans that fit
- Five or more beads
- Two colors embroidery floss and needle
- Thread for use with denim and denim needle for your machine
- One or two colors serger thread*
- Two or three colors thread
- Seam ripper

- Several images printed on fabric. For those used on the jeans cuff, *refer to the Featured Artwork section (page 9).* The image used in pocket "frame" is cut out at 3¼" wide x 3¾" high.
- Six vintage or new buttons – four should be of descending size and two that are ½" and ¾"
- A variety of medium-weight, decorator and vintage fabrics such as velvets, brocades, tapestry, bark cloth, etc.
- *Optional:* Pinking shears
- *Optional:* Fabric glue or fusible web

*A machine zigzag stitch can be substituted for serged stitching.

DISASSEMBLY AND PREPARATION OF JEANS

1. Cut off jeans legs to desired finished length. The sample shown is a slightly cropped length.

2. Using seam ripper, remove INNER seam on both legs until you can lay the lower edge of jeans relatively flat. It will be easier to work if you remove quite a bit of the seam and it is easily resewn. Finish lower edge with serging, etc. Do not hem.

3. From the left back pocket cut out a rectangle "frame" to hold image. The dimensions of the "frame" should be 2¼" wide x 2¾" high. Refer to MATERIALS NEEDED. **SEE FIG. A.**

A

ASSEMBLY INSTRUCTIONS

Read this section thoroughly before beginning.

1. Thread serger with one color that will bind the fabric strips. Thread machine with another contrasting color.

2. Open lower jeans leg out flat. Measure and record the width of lower edge. With this figure in mind, begin cutting out a variety of fabric strips, most of which should be vertical and approximately 8" tall. The widths should vary somewhat. Vary the height slightly and on some strips, cut the short ends at an angle. For some, combine two smaller pieces to make the finished height. For example a 2" and a 6" piece combined. Cut out two random, irregular shapes to appliqué on top that are approximately 1" x 1½". Cut three horizontal rectangular strips of various lengths. See photographs for reference. Serge the edges of two and pink the edges of the third. These horizontal pieces are to be overlaid on top of the vertical strips. Also, cut out a ½" x 4" strip and pink the edges. When cutting from the decorator fabrics, utilize the selvages! Many are visually interesting with different weaves and textures and can be left visible on the cuff when strips are sewn together.

3. Cut out your images. Refer to photos to give you some ideas on how to vary their placement. Slide the edges of some under a fabric strip. Pink one side of an image or cut away part of an image to reveal a detail. Use a variety of stitches around them.

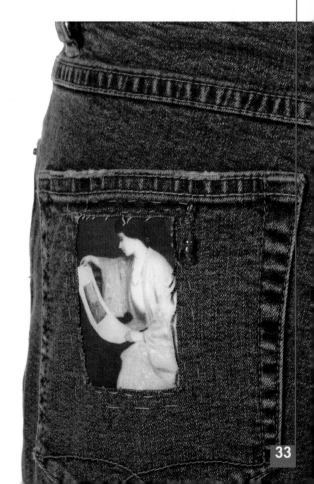

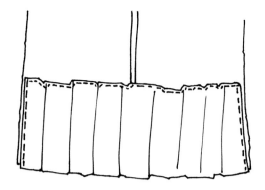

B

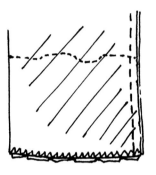

C

D

4. Begin connecting the strips and images to achieve your desired width—the measurement you recorded from the lower jeans leg in Step 2. Connect all of them by OVERLAPPING ¼". pinning and stitching together. Do not use just a straight stitch. Use your machine's decorative stitches or zigzag. The top edge should be staggered a little. The lower edge can also be staggered but should not extend below lower edge of jeans by more than about ⅜".

5. When you have finished connecting the vertical strips, refer to photos to place your horizontal pieces on top. The ½" wide strip with pinked edges was positioned vertically next to an image and attached with 3 strands of embroidery floss stitched in six large X's. The two small irregular pieces are positioned at an angle, slightly overlapping an image, and appliquéd on top. Do a running stitch of embroidery floss across some pieces, if desired. Multiple rows of horizontal decorative stitching add depth to solid fabrics, such as velvet.

6. Stitch four buttons of descending size next to each other across a horizontal band on one leg embellishment. On the other leg embellishment, stitch a pair of interesting buttons.

7. With the right sides up, make sure the completed embellishments are securely sewn to jean legs along the upper edges of the embellishment. The lower edges do not need to be stitched to jean. Baste side edges of embellishment to jean legs inside the exposed seam allowance. **SEE FIG. B.**

8. Turn jean WSO. With RST, pin along original seam line of legs. Stitch along this seam line. Press. Turn jean RSO. **SEE FIG. C.**

Center image under "frame" of left back pocket. Pin on the outside of jean. Using 3 strands of embroidery floss do a running stitch close to cut edge of denim frame in first color. Using a second color of floss, do a running stitch ¼" beyond the first stitching. On the upper right corner, stitch five

aztec accent jacket

The Aztec Accent Jacket is both artful and sophisticated. Bright bands of richly colored wool roving are needle felted in a pattern evocative of the Aztec culture or desert Southwest and applied to collar, sleeve, front and back yokes. Detailed instructions are provided to help you transform a simple denim jacket into a stunning accent piece for your wardrobe.

PREPARATION OF JEAN JACKET

1. Analyze the lines of your denim jacket. Determine where the trim will be most suitable for your jacket and body style. Placing trim centered or alongside existing seams is the simplest, but don't necessarily limit yourself to that option. Oftentimes, placement that frames the face or directs the eye up toward the face is most flattering. Adapt the following directions to vary the size and location of the trim to suit your particular jacket and preferences.

2. It is strongly recommended that you needle felt a small sample of the trim (including rinsing out the stabilizer and drying) before beginning. This will give you an idea of how much roving you must use for the trim to get good coverage that has enough body to hold together well, but not so much that the trim is excessively bulky.

MATERIALS NEEDED

- Ready-to-wear denim jacket

- Non-woven water soluble stabilizer (the fabric-like type, not the plastic-like type, is preferable)

- Wool roving in six colors (Clover Needlecraft colors featured). Sample used teal, violet, rust, orange, and moss green.

- Quick-tack fabric glue such as Beacon Fabritac

- Clover felting needle tool and mat

- Additional coarse felting needles

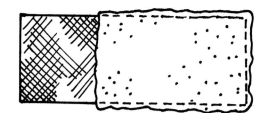

A

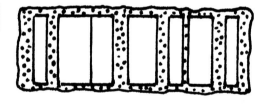

B

TRIM

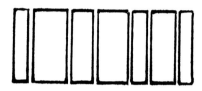

C

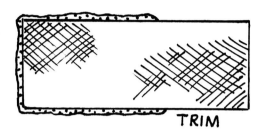

D

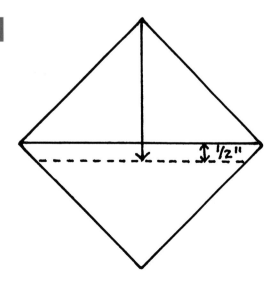

E

↕ ½"

ASSEMBLY INSTRUCTIONS

1. To determine the total length of trim needed to duplicate the jacket pictured, use the following chart:

Width of back yoke:		_____ "
Length around outside edge of collar:	+	_____ "
	+	__6__ "
Total of above:	=	_____ "

2. Cut two pieces of water-soluble stabilizer the calculated total length above by 1¼" wide. Cut one of the two lengths into five equal length segments.

3. Using the gold roving, needle felt a solid layer of roving onto the longest strip of stabilizer. The roving should completely and evenly cover the stabilizer. Make sure the roving fully covers the width, which means that there will be a small amount of roving extending beyond the edges of the stabilizer. **SEE FIG. A.**

4. Using the other five colors, repeat step 3 with each of the five shorter segments of stabilizer, using one color per strip.

5. Turn one of the shorter five strips so that the stabilizer is facing up. Trim the excess roving even with the edge of the stabilizer to the 1¼" width of the stabilizer. Repeat with the remaining four short strips. **SEE FIG. B.**

6. Take each of the five short colored strips and cut into smaller segments of random widths, varying from ¼" to ¾" wide. **SEE FIG. C.**

7. Arrange the different colored segments centered on to the long gold needle felted strip. Vary the spacing between the segments, with some segments butted together and others as much as ⅝" apart. Work in small sections and needle felt just enough to hold in place until the entire strip is arranged.

Make any adjustments to the colors and spacing and when satisfied, needle felt the segments securely in place. **SEE FIG. D.**

8. Cut the remaining small colored segments in half crosswise into ½" and ¾" high segments, keeping each size separate. Set aside.

9. Cut two 3" squares and one 4" square of water soluble stabilizer. Mark a diagonal line from corner to corner on each square. Mark a second line a ½" below the diagonal line. Needle felt gold roving from the top point of all three squares extending to the lower line, ½" beyond the diagonal mark. **SEE FIG. E.**

10. On scraps of the water-soluble stabilizer mark one 2½" square, two 2" squares, one 1½" square and one 1" square, but don't cut out just yet. On all these squares except the smallest 1" square, mark a line ½" from two adjacent edges. **SEE FIG. F.**

11. The L-shaped segment is the area that you will needle felt. Needle felt beyond the marked area so that you completely cover the L-shape of each square with roving, in the following colors:

- on the 2½" square use rust roving
- on one 2" square use violet roving
- on the second 2" square use teal roving
- on the 1½" square use violet roving
- on the smallest 1" square, needle felt the entire square with orange roving

12. Turn the stabilizer side up and on the lines previously marked, cut out the L-shapes as shown. **SEE FIG. G.**

13. Layer these colored L-shapes as shown onto the appropriate size gold square and securely needle felt in place. **SEE FIGS. H, I & J.**

14. Use the ¾" long segments from step 8 to add a striped border to the 4" medallion. Use the

F

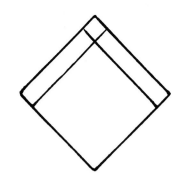

G

H

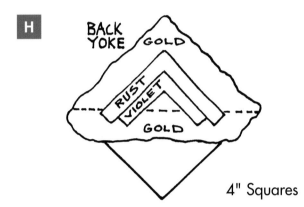

4" Squares

I

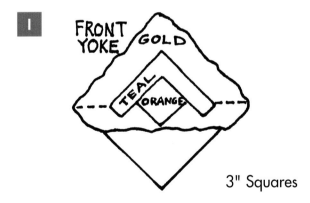

3" Squares

J

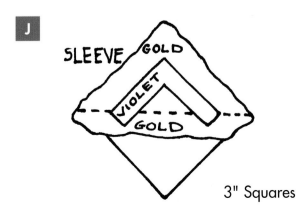

3" Squares

½" long segments from step 8 to add a striped border to the two 3" medallions. **SEE FIG. K.**

15. Check to make sure all segments are securely needle felted in place. Trim excess stabilizer on the medallions close to the felting.

16. Fill a sink or large bowl with cool water. Place the needle felted strip and the three medallions in the cool water. Make sure that all are submerged, and gently agitate and press between your fingers to make sure that the water penetrates through the layers. Let soak for 15 or 20 minutes. Drain the water, and repeat. Examine and feel the wool. You should not be able to see or feel any remaining stabilizer. If you do, repeat until no trace of the stabilizer remains.

17. Lay the wool on a bath towel and gently press out excess water. Let dry overnight.

18. Trim the three medallions on the diagonal from point to point. Lightly trim any excessively irregular edges on the long edges of the striped border strip and the medallions, leaving a softly undulating edge. **SEE FIG. L.**

19. Center the 4" medallion above the back yoke. Refer to photograph for placement. Pin in place. Test the placement of the long strip (centered over the back yoke seam) and adjust the position of the medallion so the cut edge of the medallion is covered by the long strip.

20. Remove pins from one-half of the medallion and spread a very light layer of glue on the free segment, keeping glue at least ⅛" from the outside edges. Press into place. Unpin the remaining half of the medallion and glue the remaining half in place.

21. Center the long strip over the back yoke seam, with the end of the strip extending slightly onto the sleeve. Trim the end of the strip to follow the sleeve seam line.

K
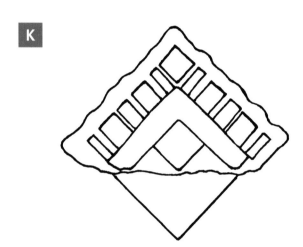

L

22. Spread a very light layer of glue on 3" of the strip, keeping glue at least a ⅛" from the long irregular edges. Press into place, centering strip over the back yoke seam. Continue gluing into place approximately 3" segments at a time. As you near the other sleeve seam, trim the strip to follow the sleeve seam line and glue into place.

23. Cut the remaining section of the long strip in half lengthwise. **SEE FIG. M.**

24. On the right front, align the cut edge of the long strip to the bottom of the front yoke seam and glue into place, wrapping the strip around the front edge of your jacket approximately ½". Refer to the photograph.

25. Align the cut edge of a 3" medallion to the bottom of the front yoke seam, centered above the pocket. Glue into place. Position the other 3" medallion on the outside of the right sleeve so that the sleeve rolls up to hide the cut edge and glue in place. Refer to the photograph.

26. On the front edges of the collar, beginning ⅝" from the point of the collar, and placing the cut edge of the wool strip approximately ¹⁄₁₆" beyond the edge of the collar, glue the first 1" section of trim in place. Holding the collar turned down as worn, wrap the strip up and around the "turn" of the collar and trim even with the collar seam on the inside. Do not lay the collar flat to measure or the strip will be too short! Glue the remainder of the strip into place and immediately squeeze the fold of the collar between your fingers (as it will be worn) until the glue dries. Refer to the photograph.

27. Glue the remaining strip to the outside edge of the collar, extending each end beyond the collar points and the long edge extending approximately ¹⁄₁₆" beyond the edge of the collar. When the glue is dry, trim ends neatly at the collar points.

28. Using coarse felting needles, needle felt the uncut edges of the medallions and strips onto the denim. Where there are seams, omit needle felting entirely. Add glue if necessary or needle felt slowly and carefully so as not to break the needles.

M

yarn medley jacket

Although shown as a woman's jacket, this is easily adapted to a child's jacket by following the directions as given. Your denim jacket's collar, pocket flaps, cuffs, etc. provide the perfect palette for a playful painting of fibers and yarns. The colorful accent flatters the face and delights both wearer and viewer. A high-end boutique look is yours at a fraction of the cost by embellishing a basic denim jacket while having fun in the process.

MODEL 1978

PREPARATION OF JEAN JACKET

1. Using a copy machine or tissue paper, copy or trace the elements of your jacket that you wish to embellish, such as the collar, cuffs and/or pocket flaps, etc. After the pattern pieces are copied from your garment cut around them leaving an additional ¼". Lay the paper pattern pieces onto your garment as you would be wearing it. The collar will curve around and down on your neck, the cuffs will curve around your wrist—this may mean additional allowances on the pattern pieces. Cut new paper pieces if needed to fit, adding an additional ½" seam allowance to all edges of your final pattern pieces. **SEE FIG. A.**

MATERIALS NEEDED

■ One denim jacket that fits – a traditional style works best

■ An assortment of yarns and threads (the sample used two different colors of perle cotton and eight different colors and textures of yarn)

■ Adhesive water soluble stabilizer* (large enough to fit all your pattern pieces on)

■ Water soluble stabilizer film* (large enough to fit to over the entire adhesive stabilizer)

■ Invisible thread

■ Heavy-duty thread to match assorted yarn

■ *Optional:* rolling pin

* Sample used Aqua Bond water soluble adhesive stabilizer and Aqua Film for the topping stabilizer.

HOW TO MAKE YOUR YARN MEDLEY FABRIC

1. Place the water soluble adhesive stabilizer face down (adhesive side up) on a flat surface. Tape the corners and sides as needed to the flat surface to keep it from moving. Peel off the paper backing, exposing the adhesive. **SEE FIG. B.**

2. You are going to make a piece of fabric from a variety of yarns, threads, ribbons, etc. Place the fibers in layers remembering the first and last layers will be the most visible on either side of your fabric. Arrange the decorative yarns and threads over the entire surface of the adhesive stabilizer. This is a great way to be creative and play! If you need to rearrange the yarns, etc., remove them and try again until you are satisfied with your design. **SEE FIG. C.**

3. When you have finally achieved the look you desire, cover the entire surface with the non-adhesive water soluble stabilizer film. Use your hands or a rolling pin to press the layers firmly together. Pin together if necessary. **SEE FIG. D.**

4. Thread your machine with invisible thread. Using a straight stitch (length: 2mm) sew around the entire outer edge of your stabilizer pieces, through all layers. Next, work from side to side, stitching a ⅜" to ½" grid over the entire surface. **SEE FIG. E.**

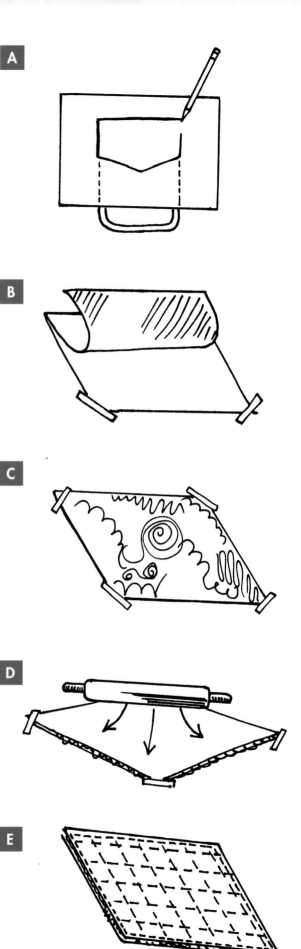

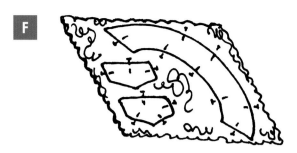

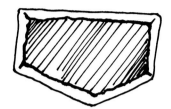

TIP: A seam guide attached to the presser foot is useful for stitching evenly-spaced parallel lines.

5. Fill a basin with warm water. Immerse the yarn medley fabric and let it sit for a minute or two. Gently swish to remove the stabilizer. Change the water and rinse again. Repeat several times until the all the stabilizer is removed and the yarn fabric does not feel sticky. Roll fabric between two towels to remove excess moisture. Lay flat to dry.

CUTTING INSTRUCTIONS

1. Pin the paper pattern pieces that you made from the collar, cuffs, etc. to the yarn medley fabric and cut them out. **SEE FIG. F.**

ASSEMBLY INSTRUCTIONS

1. Finger press the ½" seam allowance to the wrong side of the yarn fabric on each pattern piece and pin in place to the collar and the pocket flaps, etc. Line up the folded edges of the yarn pieces with the finished edge of the denim elements of your jacket. **SEE FIG. G.**

2. Using heavy-duty thread, sew a blanket stitch around the yarn fabric embellishment to attach it to your jacket. If you would like to bring out an additional color, couch a yarn on top of this fabric. **SEE FIG. H.**

3. If you have a button hole, simply work the yarn around the hole or snip a few yarns and stitch in place.

vintage rose jacket

This jacket is shown completed with a child's jacket, but it is easily adapted to a ladies' jacket following the same instructions. This is a fairly easy project for any level seamstress, and it is a great way to utilize cherished family linen with needlework. The soft, nostalgic, floral images contrast nicely with the traditional denim work-jacket style. Showcase snippets of vintage or other favorite fabrics in the bell sleeve insets and beneath the images. The chenille trims, bound together, provide textural interest and the vintage image used to replace the garment tag lends a charming quality to your garment as well.

MATERIALS NEEDED

- One denim jacket that fits

- Two colors chenille trim – approximately 1 yard each (the sample uses two shades of green)

- Three images – those used are **Baby in Tub**, **Rose in Vase** and **Rose.** *Refer to Featured Artwork section (page 9).*

- Fabric for sleeve insets – about ¼ yard for child or ⅓ yard for adult

- One large vintage textile for back. An embroidered dresser scarf with crocheted trim on each side was used for this project.

- Fabric for lower sleeve binding – about ½ yard

- Fabric for right front – approximately 5" x 8"

- Fabric for left front – approximately 5" x 12" as shown. You may need a somewhat larger piece for a larger jacket. Read instructions.

- Contrasting thread for use around images

- Seam ripper

- *Optional:* Pinking shears

- *Optional:* ½" bias tape maker

43

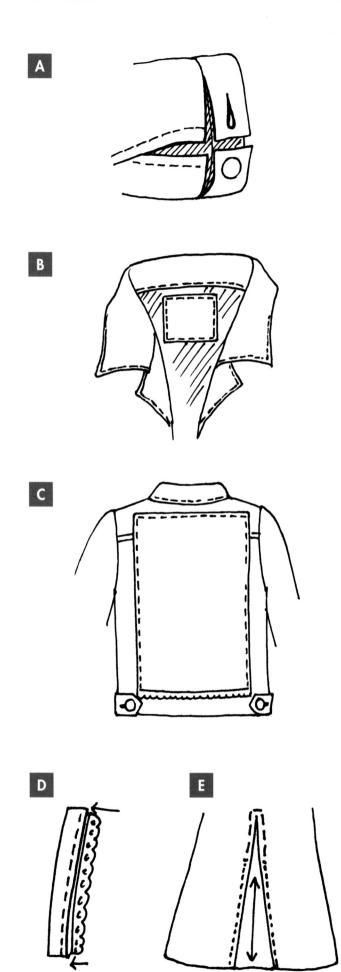

DISASSEMBLY OF JEAN JACKET

1. Cut off sleeve cuff just next to upper edge. **SEE FIG. A.**

2. With seam ripper remove underarm seam of sleeves so that opening is approximately 6" to 8" for a child or 10" to 12" for an adult jacket. Tack underarm seam at this point to keep it stable.

3. Remove any interior labels at neck. **SEE FIG. B.**

ASSEMBLY INSTRUCTIONS

NOTE: When preparing to cut out the 3 images used in this project, decide on the finished size you would like and then add ¼" to ALL sides before cutting. This extra fabric will be turned under.

1. Cut out the image (Baby in Tub) you will use as your new "label" on the interior of the jacket at the center back neck. Press under ¼" on all sides. Center image right side up just below neck seam on the wrong side of jacket back. Pin. Stitch close to folded edge all around using contrasting thread.

2. Center your vintage textile on the back of your jacket, trimming upper edge to fit, if necessary. If it has a lace or crocheted edge, leave this intact and place on the lower edge. Turn under the top edge, press and pin textile on all sides. Stitch close to outer edge with matching thread. Save any removed lace or crocheted trim with fabric attached to use for optional front pocket embellishment. **SEE FIG. C.**

3. If you have some extra lace or trim, cut two lengths that are the same width as the front vertical pockets on your jacket. Leave at least ½" of fabric attached so that you can slide this into the pocket and leave the trim peeking out. Pin and stitch to pocket. **SEE FIG. D.**

4. Lay sleeve as flat as possible with underarm seam facing up. Take measurements of the "triangle" opening you created in sleeve. To this measurement add 1" to sides and top edge of triangle. Using this new measurement cut out two triangles of fabric to use as sleeve insets. The grain line of fabric should run vertically through them. Finish all edges of inset with serging or machine finish.

5. Position the fabric inset right side up under the triangular opening of sleeve and center it. Have the lower edge of inset flush with lower cut edge of sleeve. Pin inset to sleeve on the right side, close to edge of denim. With your machine, stitch as far up as possible on both sides. If you cannot reach the top of the triangle with your machine, backstitch and resume stitching by hand with a needle and thread. You may also use two or three strands of embroidery floss if desired. **SEE FIG. E.**

6. Create a long length of ½" bias binding for the lower sleeve edge. If you have a ½" bias tape maker, follow the manufacturer's directions. If not, follow these steps:

a. Cut 2" wide strips of fabric on the bias. Stitch together as shown with ¼" seams. Press open seam allowances and trim away the small, protruding points. **SEE FIG. F.**

b. Press completed strip in half lengthwise with wrong sides together. Fold outer long edges in to meet center crease. Press again. **SEE FIG. G.**

7. To attach binding to lower sleeve follow these directions:

a. Begin at center of sleeve inset. Open out binding and with sleeve right side up, position the raw edge of sleeve in the center crease of the binding. Pin sleeve to underside of binding and stitch. **SEE FIG. H.**

b. Fold top of binding over the raw edge of sleeve to the right side (or top). **SEE FIG. I.**

c. Overlap binding at ends. Pin. Stitch close to folded edge of binding. **SEE FIG. J.**

F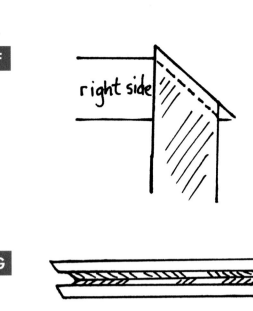
right side

G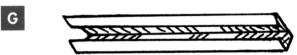

H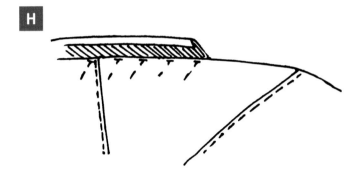

I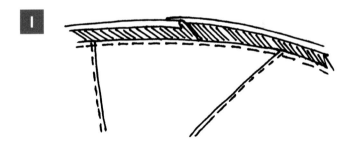

J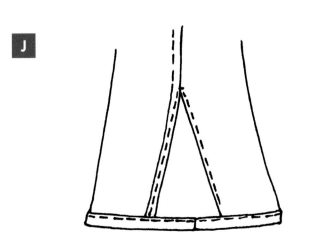

8. Cut a rectangle of decorative fabric for the right front of jacket to fit between the lower edge of the top pocket and extending just past the top of the lower waistband. See photograph. Use pinking shears, if desired, to cut around outer edges. Cut out image, making its finished size smaller than fabric rectangle. Don't forget to include the ¼" seam allowance on all sides, if needed.

9. Press under ¼" around outer edges of image. Center image on fabric rectangle and pin close to edges. Use a zigzag or decorative stitch in a contrasting color to stitch image to fabric.

10. Center this completed piece beneath right front pocket and pin. Using a contrasting thread, stitch around perimeter of fabric rectangle in a straight or decorative stitch.

11. Lift flap of left front pocket up and measure distance from the upper edge of the pocket to the upper edge of jacket lower band. Record. Measure width of pocket and record. Now cut a fabric band using these measurements. **SEE FIG. K.**

12. Cut out image to center on this fabric band. Don't forget to include the ¼" seam allowance on all sides. Make sure finished size of image is somewhat narrower than width of fabric. Press under sides of image ¼". Set aside.

13. Center the fabric band under pocket flap and determine where you would like your image. See photo. Pin image to fabric where desired. Stitch around image close to folded edge.

14. Serge or finish edges of fabric band. Center fabric band with image attached under pocket flap. Pin. Stitch close to edge down sides and lower edge.

15. Twist your two colors of chenille trim together loosely. Beginning at one upper corner of fabric band, pin one end of chenille. Continue down side, pinning as you go. Pivot at corners. When you reach the opposite top corner, trim off chenille trim. Stitch in place. **SEE FIG. L.**

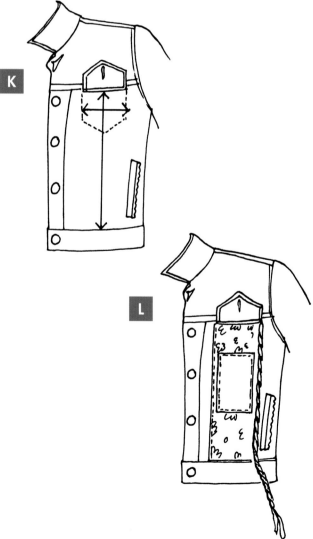

K

L

flower power ruffled jacket

The lower band of this denim jacket has been replaced with a slightly gathered band of soft fabric that is echoed again in a petite ruffle beneath the front pocket. Floral images and cherubs frolic, ribbons define and festoons of fabric combine to create a new look from an old standby— the jean jacket. The sample shown is a child's size, but it is easily adapted to a ladies' jacket by following the same instructions.

MATERIALS NEEDED

- One denim jacket that fits – a traditional style works best

- ½ yard fabric for ruffle – select a lightweight rayon, cotton or linen. Heavy fabrics are not recommended

- 1 yard ⅜" or ¼" decorative ribbon for front jacket edges (may need additional length for adult size)

- 1 yard 2½" ribbon OR 1 yard 2½" wide strip of contrasting fabric for lower jacket edge. (You may need additional length for an adult size.)

- One sheet of tracing paper or vellum and pencil

- Several images sized to fit your jacket—those used are **Rose, Rose with Cherub, Baby on Flowers,** and **Baby on Roses**. *Refer to Featured Artwork section (page 9).*

- Thread and denim needle for your machine

- *Optional:* One yard narrow trim to go around back images

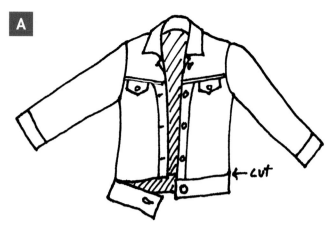

DISASSEMBLY OF JEAN JACKET

1. Cut off lower band of jacket just above upper edge of band. This will not be used. **SEE FIG. A.**

2. Remove any garment tags from inside of jacket at neck.

ASSEMBLY INSTRUCTIONS

1. Measure the length of front edge of jacket. Use this measurement to cut a length of the ⅜" or ¼" ribbon. Pin ribbon along front edges of jacket or use a LIGHT application of fabric glue to hold it in place while you stitch down each long side of ribbon. **SEE FIGS. B & C.**

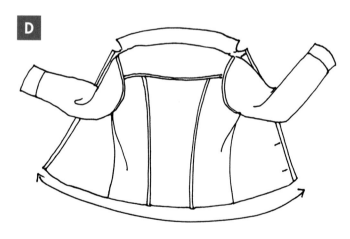

2. With measuring tape, measure the length of the lower edge of jacket from corner to corner. Add 1" to this measurement and cut a length of the 2½" ribbon or fabric this length. With WST, fold the ribbon OR the strip of fabric in half lengthwise, aligning long edges. Press. Fold in each short end ½". Press again. **SEE FIG. D.**

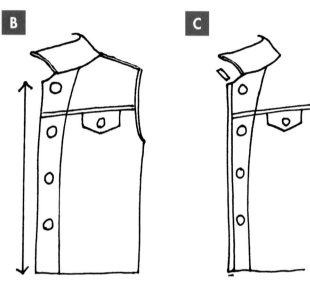

3. Beginning at one lower front corner, position folded ribbon or fabric, fold side up, along the lower raw edge of jacket. Align long edge of ribbon with lower edge of jacket and pin close to jacket edge. The folded under sections on the ends should be underneath. Stitch ¼" above lower edge of jacket. **SEE FIG. E.**

4. Now add 12" to the measurement of your lower jacket edge. For an adult jacket use one-and-a-half times the length of the lower jacket edge as the ruffle length measurement. Use this new measurement to cut a length of your ruffle fabric that is 7" wide with the grain line of the fabric vertically through it. **SEE FIG. F.**

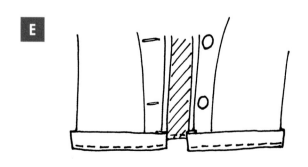

5. With RST, fold fabric in half, aligning long

edges. Pin both short ends and stitch ¼" from each end. **SEE FIG. G.**

Turn RSO. Press. Pin upper edges together and baste ½" from upper edge and again ¼" inside first stitching. **SEE FIG. H.**

Beginning at one lower front corner, with RST and gathered edge aligned with jacket lower raw edge, pin the ruffle over the ribbon, pulling up basting threads to fit until you reach the opposite lower front corner. Stitch ½" up from lower edge. Let ruffle fall down over stitching and press. **SEE FIG. I.**

6. Cut a piece of the ruffle fabric that is approximately 6" x 3". For an adult jacket use one-and-a-half times the length of the pocket opening as the ruffle length measurement. With RST, pin and stitch short side edges ¼" from edge. Turn RSO. Press. Baste across top with raw edges aligned. Pull up basting thread to gather slightly. **SEE FIG. J.**

Adjust width of ruffle so that it is the width of right front pocket. Finish raw edge and slide under right front pocket flap. Fold flap out of the way and pin and stitch ruffle beneath it so that it hangs below. **SEE FIG. K.**

7. Cut out rose for upper back. If desired, you may serge all edges of image to finish. Center on upper back and pin. Stitch close to outer edge. You may also leave edges raw before stitching, and then pin and stitch a narrow ribbon or trim centered over the outer edges of image.

8. Cut out rose with cherub image. If desired, you may serge all edges of image to finish. Center beneath upper back image and pin. Stitch close to outer edge. You may also follow directions in step 7 for trim.

9. Cut out sleeve image. Leave the left edge straight but cut in to image on the right side to define some details, such as petals. See photo. Center image on left sleeve, placing lower edge of image on upper edge of jacket cuff. Fuse to sleeve

F
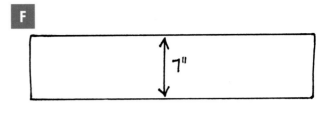
7"

G
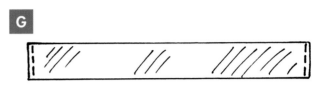

H

I
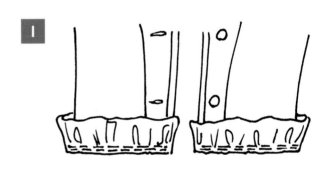

J

K
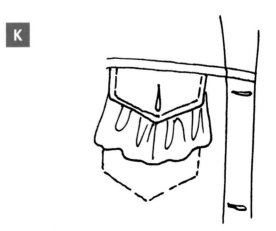

Baby on Roses

following package directions. With a contrasting thread, do a decorative machine stitch down the left and bottom side of image.

10. With tracing paper or vellum, trace upper right shoulder area of jacket above horizontal seam. See photo. Include the curve of the neck seam. After completed, draw a second set of lines that are ¼" beyond the first set. Cut along this second set of lines to use as your pattern. Pin pattern over image and cut out. Press under all edges of image ¼". Pin to upper left chest of jacket and stitch close to folded edges with matching thread.

11. Lastly, you will make a new "label" for your jacket. Cut out the rose image to specified size. Center it beneath the neck seam on interior of jacket and fuse following package directions.

whatever life sends you apron

From one pair of bib overalls you can create two delightful and versatile aprons with unlimited uses. The front of the overall will serve you well as the instigator of this apron magnifique. Wear it to your art class, host a barbeque, cook or do crafts with your kids. You can face the world in a handcrafted knockout with front fabric inset, plenty o' pockets and your treasured vintage buttons. Like we've said before, it is easily adaptable to a child-size garment by following the directions provided.

MATERIALS NEEDED

- One pair of worn denim overalls (the sample used women's Gap overalls, size medium)

- ¼ yard of fabric for bottom center insert and bib pocket flap (or other embellishment)

- ¼ yard of fabric for waist ties

- ¼ yard of fabric for neck ties

- ⅛ yard of fabric for side pocket inserts

- Scrap of medium weight interfacing for bib pocket flap (or other embellishment)

- Four 1" diameter assorted buttons

- Denim needle for machine, seam ripper, thread for use with denim

DISASSEMBLY AND PREPARATION OF OVERALLS

1. Remove the top metal buttons from both sides of the bib portion of the overalls front. We took a pair of sharp pointed scissors and trimmed around one side of the base of the metal button to loosen it from the denim, then pulled it through the hole. This will take a little strength, be patient, it will come out!

2. Using your seam ripper, rip the outer leg seams; next rip the inner leg seams. You now should have two separate front and back overalls sections. Save the back overalls section to make the **I'm Back, Bib Overalls Apron**.

3. Take the front of the overalls and rip the crotch seam up to the bottom of the faux zipper or just past the curve of the crotch seam. **SEE FIG. A.**

4. At both of the side pockets remove the stitching that holds the top of the pocket in place at the waist line, and then remove the side stitching that holds the side of the pocket in place. **SEE FIGS. B & C.**

5. Optional: If the bib portion of your overalls has a pocket flap, remove it and save it to use as a pattern piece later.

6. Your front section of your overalls is now ready to reassemble for use as an apron!

CUTTING INSTRUCTIONS FOR FABRIC

1. Using the fabric for the waist ties, cut two 4" wide by 44" long strips.

2. Using the fabric for the neck ties, cut two 4" wide by 44" long strips.

3. The fabric for the side pocket inserts will be cut out later in the instructions.

4. **Optional:** If you have a pocket flap that was removed from the bib portion of your overalls (in the previous Step #5), use it as a pattern piece and cut two fabric pieces. Don't forget to cut the ½" seam allowance.

5. Using the fabric pocket flap piece as a pattern, cut one piece from the interfacing.

ASSEMBLY INSTRUCTIONS

1. Lay the front section of the overalls on a flat surface with the wrong side facing up. Overlap the crotch seams so that the side leg seams are "almost" parallel with each other. A slight flare at the bottom of the apron is okay. With the WST, fold the two inner leg seams over; one to the right and one to the left. Create a tall triangular shaped void with the base of the triangle approximately 6" wide at about 17" down from the bottom of the faux zipper or from the top of the crotch curve. **SEE FIGS. D & E.**

2. Next, take the fabric for the bottom center insert and lay with the wrong side up, over the triangle void area, making sure to overlap the top point and both sides by at least an inch. Pin in place. **SEE FIG. F.**

3. Flip the entire front section over so that the right side is facing up; pin down each side of the triangle removing the wrong side pins so as not to sew over them. Double topstitch down each side. **SEE FIGS. G, H, & I.**

4. Trim the excess fabric and denim from the wrong side of the apron close to the triangle stitch lines.

5. Cut a fabric section from the pocket insert fabric 4½" wide by 2" longer then the length of the pocket insert section. Fold one long side of the fabric piece a ½" to the wrong side and press. With the right side up lay the folded fabric edge along the

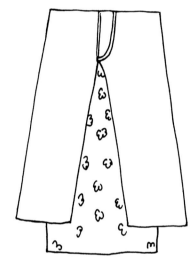

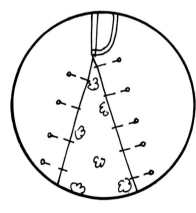

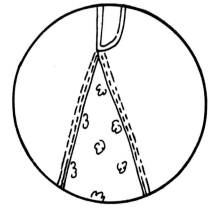

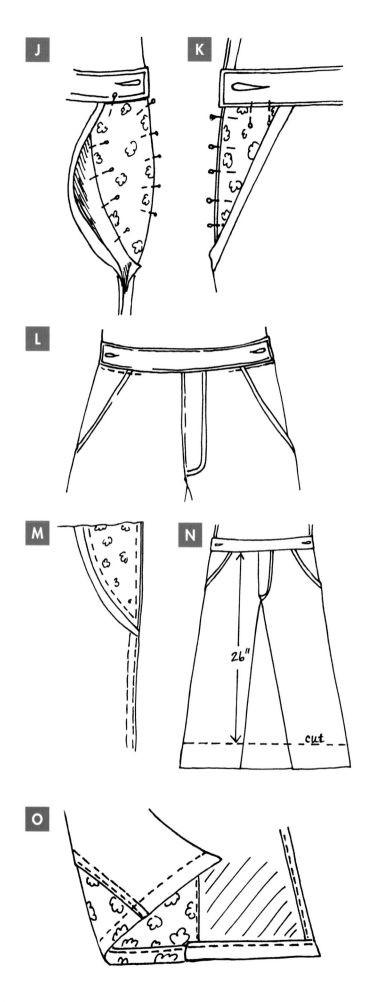

finished side edge of the denim pocket, lining up both edges and pin in place. Now fold the top raw edge of the fabric to the wrong side along the top of the denim pocket insert flush with the bottom seam of the waistband and pin in place. Tuck the remaining fabric down into the inside of the side denim pocket. You may have to trim the bottom of the fabric in order to make it fit into the bottom portion of the pocket. Topstitch close to the two folded fabric edges (side and top) and down the inside of the pocket as close to the inside raw edge as possible. Repeat for the opposite pocket. **SEE FIGS. J, K & L.**

6. Fold the raw side leg edges of the denim apron to the wrong side approximately ½" (the width of the seam allowance) and double topstitch down each apron side. Stitch waistband seam that holds top of side denim pockets back in place. **SEE FIG. M.**

7. Lay the apron on a flat surface right side up and measure down from the bottom of the waistband approximately 26" and mark across the apron bottom. Trim the bottom of the apron at your marks. This length can vary; adjust the length to your preference. **SEE FIG. N.**

8. To hem the bottom of the apron, fold to the wrong side ½" twice and topstitch close to the open edge about ¼" down from first stitch line. Set aside. **SEE FIG. O.**

9. **Optional:** If you have a pocket flap from the bib portion of your overalls, with RST and the inter-facing lying on top of the two fabrics, stitch a ½" seam allowance on all sides of the pocket flap, making sure to leave a 2" opening at the top of the fabric pocket flap for turning. If you don't have a denim pocket flap on the bib portion of your overalls, embellish the bib with fabric as you wish. Have fun with it! **SEE FIG. P.**

10. Clip the seam allowances and the corners of the flap, turn and press. Topstitch a ¼" from the bottom finished edge of the flap; backstitch at each side.

11. Center and place the fabric flap over the pocket at the location of the original denim flap. Double topstitch close to the top finished edge; backstitch at the sides. Set aside. **SEE FIG. Q.**

12. With the RST, fold one waist tie in half lengthwise and stitch down the long side using a ½" seam allowance; turn and press with the seam down the back center. Fold both ends to the inside approximately ½" and topstitch the ends closed. Repeat for the second waist tie. Set aside. **SEE FIG. R.**

13. With the RST, fold one neck tie in half lengthwise and stitch down the long side using a ½" seam allowance. Turn and press with the seam down the back center. Fold both ends to the inside approximately a ½" and topstitch the ends closed. Repeat for the second neck tie.

14. Place the end of one of the neck ties over the area where the metal button was removed from the bib portion of the overalls (the seam side of tie on the right side of the denim bib portion) approximately 1½" down from the top of the bib and stitch in place. Repeat for the second neck tie. **SEE FIG. S.**

15. Place the end of one of the waist ties under the top button hole at the side of the overalls (the right side of tie on the wrong side of the denim overalls) approximately 2" in from the finished side of the apron and stitch in place. Repeat for the second waist tie. **SEE FIGS. T & U.**

16. Sew one of the buttons at the end of the neck tie where the metal button was previously. Repeat for opposite side. **SEE FIG. V.**

17. Sew one of the buttons at the end of the waist tie over the exposed button hole. Repeat for opposite side. **SEE FIG. W.**

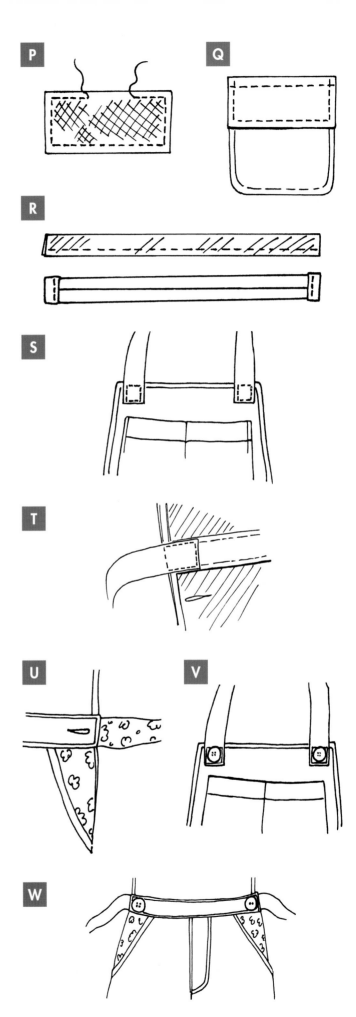

I'm back, bib overalls apron

From a pair of bib overalls you can create two charming aprons with endless possibilities. The back of the overall serves as the basis for this slimming rendition. A parade of vintage buttons march across the top and fabric accents rest beneath the patch pockets. One of the overall's pockets has been replaced with one in a contrasting print fabric, and yet another fabric provides ties. No need to hide it away when not in use as it is charming to view when hanging from a peg or hook in your abode. It may easily be adapted to a child-size overalls by following the directions given.

MATERIALS NEEDED

- One pair of worn denim overalls (the sample used women's Gap overalls, size medium)

- ½ yard of fabric for bottom center insert and the waist ties

- ¼ yard of fabric for replacement pocket

- ⅛ yard of fabric for pocket patches

- 10" square of medium weight interfacing (for the replacement pocket)

- Ten ¾" diameter assorted buttons

- Denim needle for machine, seam ripper, thread for use with denim

DISASSEMBLY AND PREPARATION OF OVERALLS

1. First remove the overalls hardware from the shoulder straps.

2. Using your seam ripper, rip the outer leg seams; next rip the inner leg seams. You now should have two separate front and back overalls sections. Save the front overalls section to make the **Whatever Life Sends You Apron**.

3. Take the back of the overalls and rip the crotch seam up to the bottom edge of the back pockets, past the curve of the crotch.

4. Remove the left back pocket; save the pocket to use as a pattern piece. **SEE FIG. A.**

5. Rip the side seams of the right back pocket approximately 2" down from the top finished edge of the pocket and leave for later instructions. **SEE FIG. B.**

6. Your back overalls section is now ready to reassemble for use as an apron!

CUTTING INSTRUCTIONS FOR FABRIC

1. Using the fabric for the waist ties, cut two 4" wide by 44" long strips.

2. Using the fabric for the pocket patches, cut two 4" by 9" pieces.

3. Using the fabric for the replacement pocket, use the denim back pocket that was removed from the overalls as a pattern piece and cut two pattern pieces. Don't forget to cut the ½" seam allowance. **SEE FIG. C.**

4. Using the replacement pocket as a pattern, cut one piece from the interfacing.

A
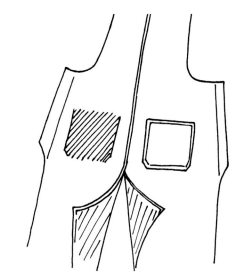

B

C

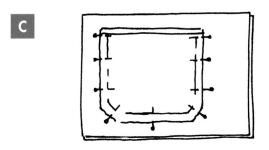

ASSEMBLY INSTRUCTIONS

1. Lay the back section of the overalls on a flat surface with the wrong side facing up. Overlap the crotch seams so that the side leg seams are "almost" parallel with each other (a slight flare at the bottom of the apron is okay). With the WST, fold the two inner leg seams over; one to the right and one to the left creating a tall triangle void with the base of the triangle approximately 6" wide at about 14" down from the bottom of the back pockets. **SEE FIG. D.**

2. Next, take the remaining piece of the waist tie fabric and lay it with the wrong side up over the triangle void area, making sure to overlap the top point and both sides by at least an inch. Pin in place. **SEE FIG. E.**

3. Flip the entire back section over so that the right side is facing up; pin down each side of the triangle (remove the wrong side pins so as not to sew over them). Double topstitch down each side. **SEE FIGS. F, G AND H.**

4. Trim the excess fabric and denim from the wrong side of the apron close to the triangle stitch lines. **SEE FIG. I.**

5. Fold the raw side leg edges of the denim apron to the wrong side approximately ½" (the width of the seam allowance) and double topstitch down each apron side. **SEE FIG. J.**

6. Lay the apron on a flat surface right side up and measure down from one side approximately 26" and mark. Do the same for the opposite side. Lining up your marks, trim the bottom of the apron. This length can vary; adjust the length to your preference. **SEE FIG. K.**

7. To hem the bottom of the apron, fold to the wrong side a ½" twice and topstitch close to the open edge and again about ¼" down from first stitch line. Set aside. **SEE FIG. L.**

8. With RST and the interfacing lying on top of the two fabrics, stitch a ½" seam allowance on all sides of the replacement pocket, making sure to leave a 2" opening at the bottom of the pocket for turning.

9. Clip the seam allowances and the corners of the pocket, turn and press. Topstitch a ¼" from the top finished edge of the pocket; backstitch at each side. Set aside.

10. Take the two pocket patch pieces and press ½" to the wrong side of the fabric on all four sides of each fabric patch. SEE FIG. M.

11. Center and place one pocket patch under the top section of the existing denim pocket that is still partially attached. The top of the pocket patch should be about 1¼" from the top of the denim pocket when the pocket is folded back up in its original place. Fold the top section of the denim pocket back down and pin it out of the way. Topstitch close to the finished edge of the pocket patch on all four sides. SEE FIG. N.

12. Unfold the denim pocket back into its original position and double topstitch the sides close to the finished edge; backstitch at the top for reinforcement. SEE FIG. O.

13. For reference only, place the completed fabric pocket over the area where the back denim pocket was completely removed and pin in place. Center and place the remaining pocket patch under the top section of this fabric pocket. The top of the pocket patch should be about 1¼" from the top of the fabric pocket when the pocket is folded back up in its place. Fold the top section of the fabric pocket back down and pin it out of the way. Topstitch close to the finished edge of the patch on all four sides.

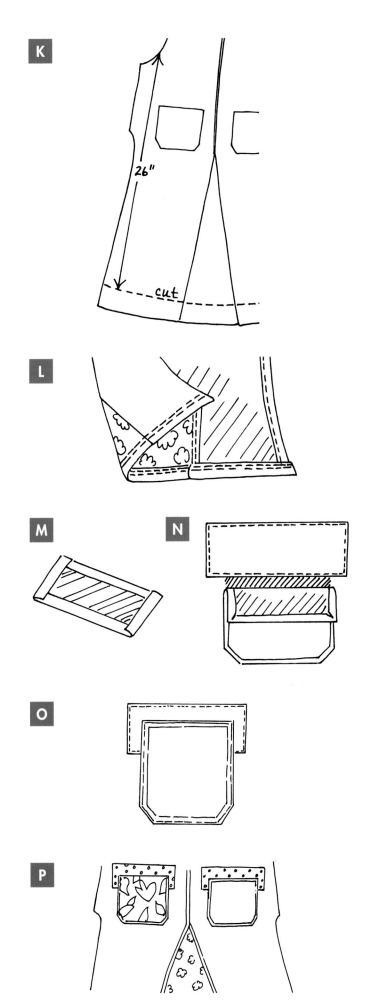

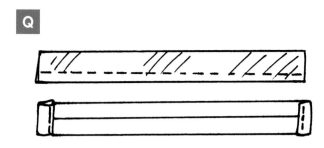

Q

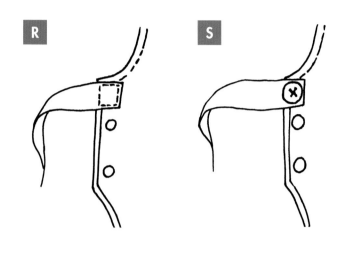

R **S**

14. Unfold the fabric pocket back into its original position and double topstitch the sides and bottom close to the finished edge; backstitch at the top for reinforcement. Set aside. **SEE FIG. P.**

15. With the RST, fold one waist tie in half lengthwise and stitch down the long side using a ½" seam allowance. Turn and press with the seam down the back center. Fold both ends to the inside approximately ½" and topstitch the ends closed. Repeat for the second waist tie. **SEE FIG. Q.**

16. Remove the top metal buttons only from both sides of the overalls apron. We took a pair of sharp pointed scissors and trimmed around one side of the base of the metal button to loosen it from the denim, then pulled it through the hole. This will take a little strength, be patience, it will come out!

17. Place the end of one of the waist ties over the area where the top metal button was removed (the seam side of tie on the right side of denim apron) and stitch in place. Repeat for the second waist tie. **SEE. FIG. R.**

18. Sew one of the buttons at the end of the waist tie where the metal button was previously located. Repeat for opposite side. **SEE. FIG. S.**

19. Sew the remaining six buttons horizontally onto the top edge of the apron bib portion. Refer to the photograph for placement. This step is for decoration only. Use your creativity and embellish your apron as you wish!

be still my heart utility apron

You're going to LOVE all the ways you can use this sassy little apron. Constructed from the back of a pair of jeans, the two pockets provide a handy receptacle for whatever your heart desires; fix-it tools, paint brushes, cleaning supplies, cooking utensils, craft supplies, gardening tools and anything else that floats your boat. If you want to be REALLY hip, add the vintage tie and button embellishment to one pocket. A vintage tie wraps itself around your waist and ties in back to secure.

MATERIALS NEEDED

- One pair of worn denim jeans (the sample used men's Levi's, size 35)
- Three vintage men's ties
- One 1¼" diameter button
- Denim needle for machine, seam ripper, thread for use with denim

DISASSEMBLY OF JEANS

1. First, cut the legs off the jeans approximately 12" down from the inner crotch seam.

2. Using your seam ripper, rip the inner double seams open first, then rip the outer single seams open up to the waistband.

3. With seam ripper, remove the waistband from the front side of the jeans only at the waistband seam. You will also have to remove the belt loops from the front side in order to remove the waist-

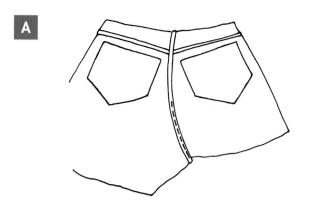

A

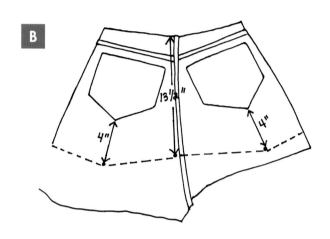

B

13½"
4"
4"

band. Keep the belt loops and waistband intact on the back side of the waistband.

4. Trim the sides of the waistband flush with the extended raw side seams.

5. The front and the back of the jeans are now separated. Save the front side of the jeans to make the **My Way Jean Front Apron.**

6. Rip the side seams of one of the back pockets approximately 2" down from the top of the pocket and leave for later instructions.

7. Take the back of the jeans and rip the crotch seam up past the bottom edge of the pockets and just past the curve of the bottom.

8. Your jeans are now ready to reassemble.

9. Lay the back of the jeans, right side up, on a flat surface. Take the upper crotch seam and lay it over the under crotch seam, creating a flat fabric surface and a straight back seam. Pin in place. **SEE FIG. A.**

10. Topstitch this crotch seam onto the opposite crotch seam.

CUTTING INSTRUCTIONS

1. With the back of your jeans lying right side up on a flat surface, measure and place marks approximately 13½" down from the top edge of the waistband.

2. Next, measure and place marks approximately 4" down from the bottom right and left edges of the two back pockets. **SEE FIG. B.**

3. Following these marks, trim the bottom edge of your tool belt. This allows for a ½" hem allowance.

4. **Optional:** This is just one suggestion for cutting and finishing the bottom edge of your utility apron. You can hem your tool belt any way or any length you please or just leave it with a raw edge.

ASSEMBLY INSTRUCTIONS

1. Press a ½" hem to the wrong side of the denim utility apron at the bottom edge and both sides. Topstitch in place. Set aside.

2. Decide which of the men's ties you will be using for the waistband and the top edge of the ripped pocket. The waist tie should probably be the longest tie. With your seam ripper remove the back seam of both of these ties that you have chosen to use and press open.

3. Take the one tie you are using for the waist-band and fold it in half lengthwise, with RST. Starting at the narrow end of the tie with a ½" seam allowance, stitch the opening closed parallel to the folded edge. This will make the tie one continuous width the entire length of the tie. Trim excess seam allowance and turn inside out. Press the tie with the seam located down the center back side of the tie. Set aside. **SEE FIGS. C & D.**

4. Take the tie you are using for the top edge of the pocket (that you removed the stitching on in Step 6 of the Disassembly of Jeans section above) and at the narrow end of the tie, cut a section 2" wider than the top width of the back pocket.

5. With RST, center and place the tie section onto the unstitched portion of the back pocket with the raw edge approximately ¾" down from the top edge of the pocket. Stitch a ½" seam allowance. Make sure that when you fold the wrong side of the tie up and over and tight to the top finished edge of the pocket, that it extends down at least 1" into the inside of the pocket. If not, make necessary adjustments. **SEE FIG. E.**

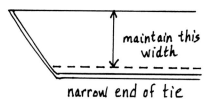

C

maintain this width

narrow end of tie

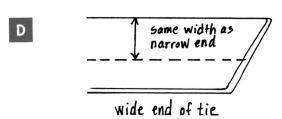

D

same width as narrow end

wide end of tie

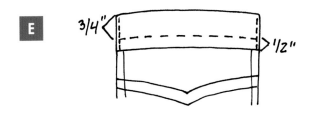

E

3/4" ½"

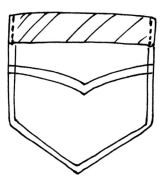
F

G

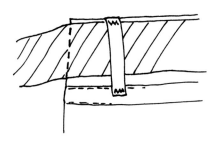
H

raw edge of tie
is placed 2"
inside pocket
2"

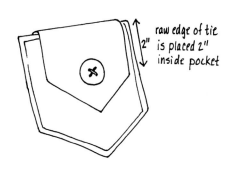
I

6. With WST, fold the sides of the tie section to the inside of the pocket and pin in place.

7. Next, fold the tie section up and over the pocket's top finished edge. Pin the pocket back in place and topstitch the side seams. Backstitch at the beginning of the seam to reinforce the pocket's opening. **SEE FIG. F.**

8. With the third and remaining tie, cut approximately 6" off the wider end of the tie.

9. With WST, center and insert the raw edge of the tie down into the remaining back pocket approximately 2". If necessary, adjust the length you want exposed to the outside. Stitch across the top edge of the pocket, catching the tie. This stitch is kind of tricky since the pocket is still attached to the back of the jeans, but it can be done. Be patient! Fold the tie down over the top edge of the pocket and secure with a button. Make sure not to sew the button through to the inside of the jeans. You want to be able to use the pocket! **SEE FIG. G & H.**

10. Weave the waistband tie through the existing belt loops, center and secure in place by stitching the tie to the sides of the existing waistband. **SEE FIG. I.**

my way jean front apron

Do it your way and assemble a medley of favorite fabrics, a few special buttons and the front of an old pair of jeans to create this easy-to-make piece. Fun and youthful with fully functional pockets, it is definitely not your mother's apron.

DISASSEMBLY OF JEANS

1. First, cut the legs off the jeans approximately 12" down from the inner crotch seam.

2. Using your seam ripper, rip the inner double seams open first, then rip the outer seams open up to the waist band.

3. Remove the waist band from the front side of the jeans only at the seam. You will also have to remove the belt loops from the front side in order to remove the waistband.

4. The front and the back of the jeans are now separated. Save the back side of the jeans with the waistband intact to make the **Be Still My Heart Utility Apron**.

5. Take the front of the jeans and rip the crotch seam up to the bottom end of the zipper.

6. Your jeans are now ready to reassemble.

MATERIALS NEEDED

- One pair of worn denim jeans (the sample used men's Levi's, size 34)
- ⅓ yard of fabric for waistband/ties
- ⅛ yard of fabric for side bindings
- ⅛ yard of fabric for the bottom section
- Three ¾" dia. assorted buttons
- Denim needle for machine, seam ripper, thread for use with denim

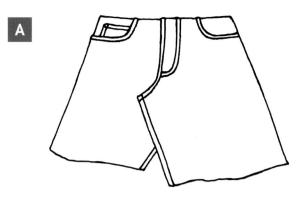

A

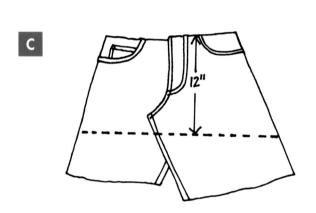

B

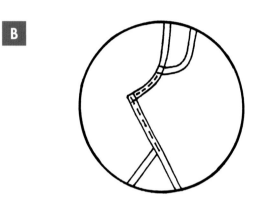

C

12"

D

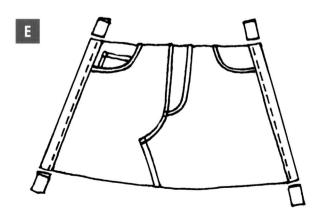

E

7. Lay the front of the jeans, right side up, on a flat surface. Take the upper crotch seam and lay it over the under crotch seam, creating a flat surface and pin in place. **SEE FIG. A.**

8. Topstitch this crotch seam onto the opposite crotch seam. **SEE FIG. B.**

CUTTING INSTRUCTIONS

1. With the front of your jeans lying right side up on a flat surface, measure and place marks approximately 12" down from the top raw edge of the jeans and cut off straight across front. **SEE FIG. C.**

2. Cut two 6" wide by approximately 44" long strips from the waistband/ties fabric.

3. Cut two 4" wide by approximately 22" long strips from side binding fabric.

4. Cut one 4" wide by approximately 44" long strip from bottom section fabric.

ASSEMBLY INSTRUCTIONS FOR FABULOUS FABRIC UTILITY APRON

1. With WST, fold one of the side binding strips in half lengthwise and press. Unfold and fold the two side raw seams into the center aligning with the center fold and press. Fold the entire length over again and press. Repeat for the second side binding strip.

2. Center and place one of the side binding strips along one side of the front denim utility apron. Encasing the raw edge of the denim inside the folded side binding strip approximately ½". Pin in place and topstitch close to the open edge. Trim off the excess binding fabric flush with the top and bottom raw edge of the utility belt. Repeat for the second side binding strip. **SEE FIGS. D & E.**

3. Sew the two waistband/tie strips together to create one long strip. **SEE FIGS. F & G.**

4. With WST, fold the waistband/tie strip in half lengthwise and press. Unfold and fold the two side raw seams into the center aligning with the center fold and press. Fold the entire length over again and press.

5. Center and place the waistband/tie strip along the top raw edge of the front denim utility apron. Placing the top raw edge inside the folded waistband strip approximately ½", pin in place and topstitch close to the open edge for the entire length of the waistband/tie strip. **SEE FIG. H.**

6. Fold one end of the waist tie ½", twice, and stitch. Repeat for opposite end of tie.

7. With RST, center and place the bottom section fabric onto the bottom raw edge of the utility apron, aligning the two raw edges. Stitch a ½" seam allowance. Unfold and press seam down toward bottom of apron.

8. Trim the excess fabric from both sides leaving approximately 2" from side binding. **SEE FIG. I.**

9. Fold one side of the bottom section to the wrong side 1" twice, aligning with side binding then stitch close to open edge. Repeat for the opposite side of the bottom section. **SEE FIG. J.**

10. To hem the bottom section, fold to the wrong side ½" twice and topstitch close to the open edge. **SEE FIG. K.**

11. Stitch three buttons vertically in place next to side binding at the top corner of one of the front pockets. Refer to photograph for location.

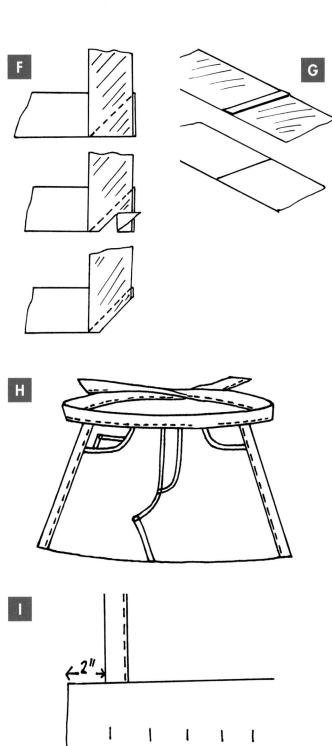

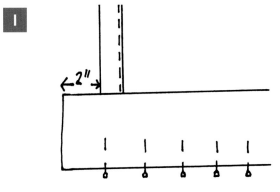

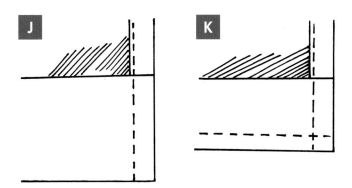

two-pocket tote

You're undeniably clever in the eyes of all who see your two-pocket tote. Construct this great medium-sized bag that's both fashionable and functional. The back pockets of your jeans, when stitched to the outside of your tote, provide the perfect place to stow your phone, keys and other essentials. The unique waistband closure with stacked vintage buttons punctuates this fabulous redesign. The finished size is 10" high by 13" wide, excluding handle.

MATERIALS NEEDED

- One pair of worn denim jeans (the sample used men's Levi's, size 38)*

- ⅓ yard of fabric for the lining and inner pocket

- Two 1¼" diameter assorted buttons (no larger than the width of the waistband)

- Two ¾" diameter assorted buttons for stacking on top of larger buttons

- Denim needle for machine, seam ripper, thread for use with denim

* Larger men's denim jeans work better for this project because the legs are wider and the pockets are larger. Also the larger the waist size is, the longer the handle. Our waistband used for this project was 39" long removed from size 38" waist jeans. If you use smaller size jeans, you will need to adjust the length of the handle accordingly.

DISASSEMBLY OF JEANS

1. Cut both legs off the jeans approximately 10½" up from the bottom finished hem of pants. **SEE FIG. A.**

2. Next, cut down the center of the back side of each leg portion. Set aside. **SEE FIG. B.**

3. Using your seam ripper, remove both back pockets from the jeans. Set aside.

4. Detach belt loops from waistband and remove waist band from jeans. Set aside.

5. Save four of the belt loops to use later.

CUTTING INSTRUCTIONS

1. Unfold each leg portion, with the hem at the top and with RST, and place each leg portion on top of the other, lining up the existing seams. Trim the width of the purse to approximately 14" wide, making sure the existing seams are equally spaced from the sides. Set aside. **SEE FIG. C.**

2. For purse lining, cut two pieces 11" high by 14" wide from lining fabric.

3. For pocket lining, cut two pieces 7" high by 9" wide from lining fabric.

ASSEMBLY INSTRUCTIONS

1. With RST and hemmed edges at the top, stitch a ½" seam allowance on both sides of the purse, leaving the bottom open. Press seams open, then turn purse so that the right side is out.

2. Center one pocket on side seam approximately 3" down from top hemmed edge and pin in place. Topstitch pocket to side of purse, leaving top of pocket open. Backstitch at top edges for extra reinforcement. Repeat for second pocket. **SEE FIG.D.**

A

B

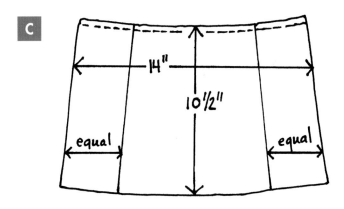

C

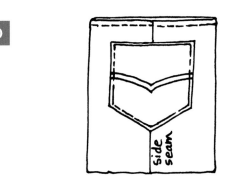

D

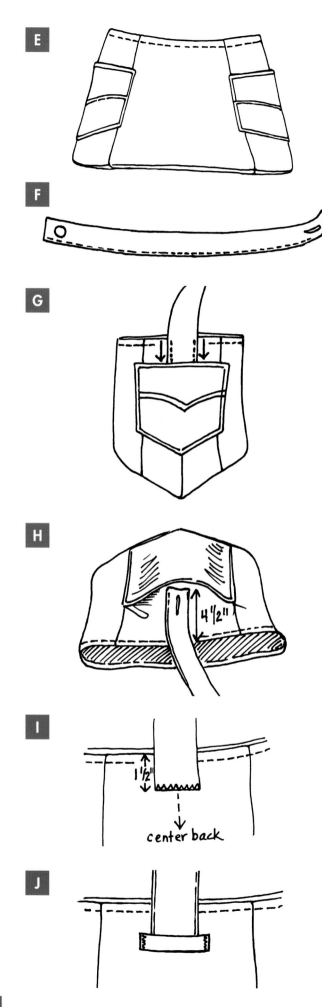

E

F

G

H

I

center back

J

3. Turn purse wrong side out, and with RST stitch bottom closed, using a ½" seam allowance. Again turn purse right side out. Set aside. **SEE FIG. E.**

4. Stitch the long open edge closed on the waistband piece, following the existing stitching line. **SEE FIG. F.**

5. The waist band used for this project was 39" long as removed from size 38" waist jeans. Cut 6" off the button end of the waistband and set aside for the flap closure. This will leave a 33" long piece from the waistband for the handle.

6. Place one end of the waistband handle piece on to the side seam; the end of the handle should be approximately 4½" down from the finished top hemmed edge of purse. The handle's end will extend down into pocket about 1½". Pin in place. Repeat for opposite end of handle, being careful not to twist the handle. Adjust the length if necessary. Topstitch both handle ends in place. **SEE FIGS. G & H.**

7. Remove the metal button from the 6" waistband piece that will be used for the closure flap. We took a pair of sharp pointed scissors and trimmed around one side of the base of the metal button to loosen it from the denim, then pulled it through the hole. This will take a little strength, be patient, it will come out!

8. Place the raw end of the 6" closure flap on to the center back of the purse, approximately 1½" down from the top of the purse; topstitch close or zigzag across the raw edge. **SEE FIG. I.**

9. Place one of the belt loops horizontally and centered over the raw edge end of the closure flap on the back of the purse, and topstitch each end of the belt loop in place, concealing the exposed raw edge of the closure flap. **SEE FIG. J.**

10. Stack two of the buttons as you prefer and sew on to the finished free end of the closure flap, concealing the hole where the metal button was. Make sure that the buttons you use are not larger than the width of the waistband, or they will not pull through the belt loop that you are going to attach next.

11. Place another belt loop on to the front of the purse, horizontally and approximately 2" down from top edge of purse. Adjust this location as needed per the location of the buttons on the closure flap when it is flipped to the front of the purse. Topstitch each end of the belt loop in place. **SEE FIG. K.**

12. Stack the remaining two buttons; center and sew on top of the belt loop attached to the back of the purse. This is simply for decoration; you could eliminate this step, if you like. **SEE FIG. L.**

13. Place the two remaining belt loops horizontally on either side of the purse, over the handle, 2" above the top of the pocket and 1" down from the top of the purse, and stitch each end of the belt loops. This is also for decoration! **SEE FIG. M.**

ASSEMBLY INSTRUCTIONS FOR LINING AND INTERIOR POCKET

1. For the pocket, with RST, stitch all four sides using a ½" seam allowance, making sure to leave a 2" opening at the bottom edge for turning.

2. Clip corners of pocket, turn inside out through opening and press.

3. Center pocket on the right side of one of the lining pieces of fabric. Stitch sides and bottom and down the center, creating two small pockets. Make sure to backstitch at the top of the pocket for extra reinforcement.

4. For the lining, with RST and the interior pocket opening located at the top, stitch the sides and the bottom using a ½" seam allowance. Clip corners and press seams open.

5. Press to the wrong side a ½" hem around the top raw edge of the lining.

6. With WST, insert the lining into the purse, aligning the top edges and pin. Handstitch around the top of the purse using a blind stitch to secure the lining to the purse.

K
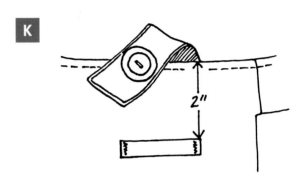

L
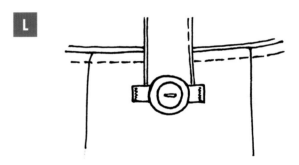

M
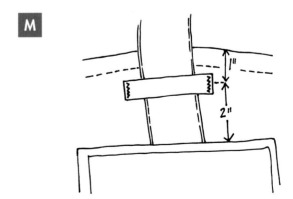

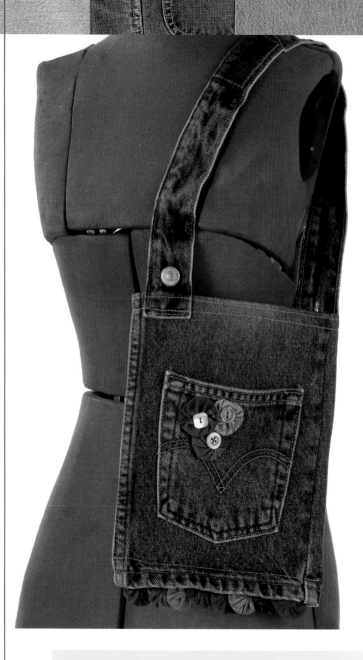

one-pocket yo-yo bag

A truly unique bag with clever detailing, constructed from a child's jean leg. The lower hem cradles a garden of fabric yo-yos in a plethora of prints. The easy access pocket is festooned with a cluster of yo-yos as well. The strap, fashioned from the jeans waistband, slips over the shoulder for a just right fit on your body.

DISASSEMBLY OF JEANS

1. First, cut the right leg off the jeans approximately 10¾" up from the bottom finished hem of leg. With your seam ripper, rip open the outer seam of this pant leg portion (the seam that is not double stitched). You will have to rip a portion of the bottom hem on either side of this seam in order to rip the bottom portion of the seam. Set aside. **SEE FIG. A.**

2. Using your seam ripper, remove one of the back pockets. Refer to Step 9 under the Assembly Instructions. Set aside.

3. For the purse handle, detach the belt loops first, and then remove the waist band from the jeans. Set aside.

MATERIALS NEEDED

- One pair of worn child's denim jeans (the sample used child's Levi's, size 10*)

- Three assorted buttons

- 11 to 12 1½" diameter yo-yos made with Clover Needlecraft Small Yo-Yo Maker *(If not using the Clover Yo-Yo Maker, instructions on how to make yo-yos are provided in the **Yarn Swirl Jeans** project.)*

- Denim needle for machine, seam ripper, thread for use with denim

* Children's denim jeans work better for this project, because the legs are not as wide and the pockets are smaller.

ASSEMBLY INSTRUCTIONS

1. Unfold and lay the denim leg portion out on a flat surface, with the right side facing up. Center and place the previously removed back pocket onto the right side section of the leg, approximately 3½" down from the top raw edge and pin in place. Topstitch, leaving the top of the pocket open. Backstitch at the top of the pocket for extra reinforcement. **SEE FIG. B.**

2. With RST, stitch the original side seam closed, following the existing side seam line. You will then have to stitch the bottom hem back in place. Set aside. **SEE FIG. C & D.**

3. On the waistband piece stitch the long open edge closed, following the existing stitching line. Set aside.

4. To finish the top edge of the purse, fold the top raw edge of the pant leg to the inside (the wrong side) approximately ¾", press and pin in place. Do not stitch at this time.

5. Place the button end of the waistband piece on to the front left corner, approximately 1" down from top edge. Pin in place. **SEE FIG. E.**

6. Place the buttonhole end of the waistband piece on to the back right corner, approximately 1" down from top edge. Pin in place. Make sure not to twist the handle. **SEE FIG. F.**

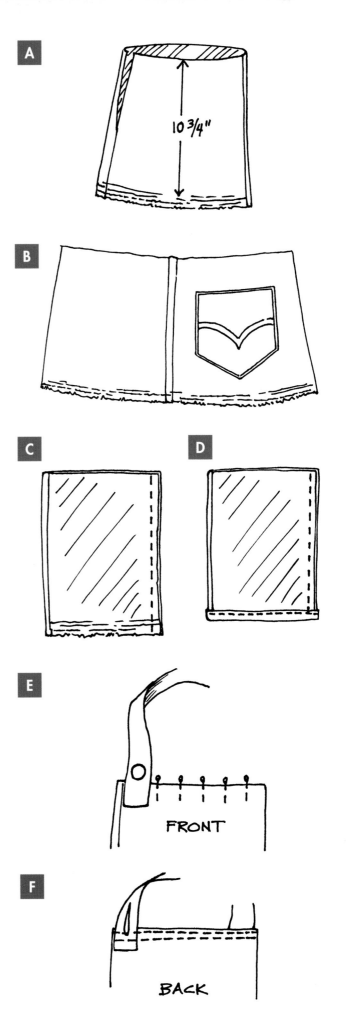

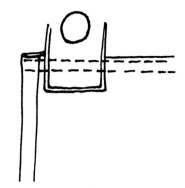

G

7. Topstitch around top of purse ⅛" down from the top edge, catching handle ends in stitching. Then topstitch again about ¼" down from first stitching. **SEE FIG. G.**

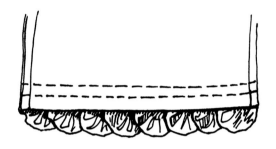

H

8. Take 8 or 9 fabric yo-yos, align horizontally and place inside opening at bottom hem of purse, leaving yo-yos half exposed and pin. Stitch bottom closed, catching yo-yos in stitching. **SEE FIG. H.**

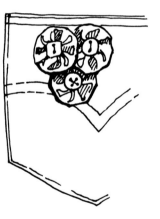

I

9. Arrange three yo-yos and three assorted buttons onto top right corner of front pocket. Refer to photograph for placement. Stitch in place. You could do this step before you attach the pocket to the purse. **SEE FIG. I.**

pocket collage

A creatively embellished pocket, front and center, defines this shoulder bag's character. (It is also adept at holding your phone.) Proudly exhibit this manner of constructing a handbag from a cast off jeans leg. The raw upper edge contrasts nicely with the prim cotton ruffle descending from the lower edge. Sling it across your shoulder and head out with a bag sized perfectly for a day's outing of shopping, flea marketing or browsing galleries. The finished size of this bag is 10" high with a 1¼" ruffle. The strap is as long as the jean waistband you choose to use.

MATERIALS NEEDED

- One pair denim jeans with straight legs and back pockets. You will use the waistband as the shoulder strap, so remember that the larger sized jeans will give you a longer strap.

- 24" x 2¼" section of fabric for lower ruffle. The sample uses vintage feedsack fabric.

- Scrap of fabric for pocket collage. The sample uses vintage bark cloth.

- Small assortment of beads

- Seam ripper and denim needle for your machine

- Two or three thread colors, thread for use with denim

- Two colors embroidery floss and needle

- Five images printed on any printable fabric. Those used are **Ferris Wheel, Atlantic City, Japanese Lanterns, Map** and **Riviera**. *Refer to Featured Artwork section (page 9).*

- One sheet of paper and pencil

- *Optional:* Pinking shears

- *Optional:* Fray Check®

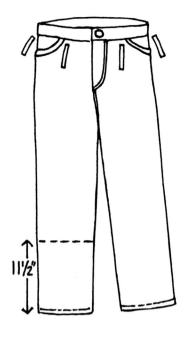

A

B

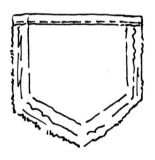

C

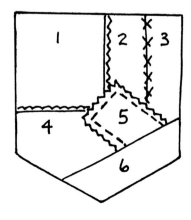

D

11½"

DISASSEMBLY OF JEANS

1. Measure up 11½" from lower edge of one jeans leg. Mark here and cut straight across leg. With seam ripper, remove OUTER single seam of leg.

2. With seam ripper, remove belt loops from jeans. They will NOT be used. **SEE FIG. A.**

3. Remove waistband totally intact from jeans by beginning at zipper and cutting just next to lower edge of waistband all around. Set aside. **SEE FIG. B.**

4. With seam ripper, remove ONE back pocket from jeans. Leave upper hem of pocket in place but unfold the side and lower hem fabric and press flat. **SEE FIG. C.**

ASSEMBLY INSTRUCTIONS

1. Create a pattern piece to make your pocket collage. Place your pocket on the sheet of paper and trace around it with a pencil. Cut out this shape. From each edge of this shape, cut away ½" of paper. You will use this as a size–guide for your collage.

2. Create the collage for your pocket. It need not be exactly like the one shown. Have fun arranging your fabric, photos and beads. Use the illustration as a guide. We will refer to each section of the collage by its corresponding illustration number. As the illustration shows, section 4 is a piece of vintage fabric while the remaining sections are images printed on fabric. All collage edges are left unfinished. You may lightly apply Fray Check to edges when completed, if desired. **SEE FIG. D.**

3. First, pin together sections 1, 2 and 3. Section 3 overlaps section 2 one-quarter of an inch and section 2 overlaps section 1 one-quarter of an inch. Use a decorative or zigzag stitch to connect them. When connected, they should cover approximately the top half of the pocket collage shape.

4. Pin together section 4 and 6 to fill the remaining space of the pocket collage shape. Slide the upper edge of sections 4 and 6 slightly under the lower edge of the top section and pin. Stitch across with decorative stitching.

5. Cut out section 5 with pinking shears and slide one end under section 6 as shown. Re-pin and stitch across with decorative stitching. Using three strands of embroidery floss, do a running stitch around the perimeter of section 5 to attach it to collage. If desired, stitch on a few beads randomly across the collage.

6. Trim any edges of completed collage, so that it fits the paper pattern you made. Center collage on pocket. Use a decorative or zigzag stitch to attach collage to pocket. Position completed pocket on the bag to the right of seam. Lower edge of pocket should be near hem of jeans leg. Pocket should not be within the exposed seam allowance. Pin. Stitch around sides and lower edge of pocket using thread for use with denim. Two rows of stitching may be used that are ¼" apart, if desired. **SEE FIG. E.**

7. With RST, align open side edges of bag that was previously the outer seam of jeans leg. Pin. Stitch along original stitching line. Turn bag RSO and press.

8. Fold top edge of bag (the cut edge) to OUTSIDE 1½". Press folded edge. Using three strands of embroidery floss, stitch two rows of a running stitch around the top of bag through the folded section. Space them about ½" apart, starting ¼" away from the lower raw edge. Use two different colors of floss, if desired. **SEE FIG. F.**

9. For the lower ruffle, turn under ¼" twice, on one long side of your fabric. Press and pin. Machine stitch close to inner fold of hem.

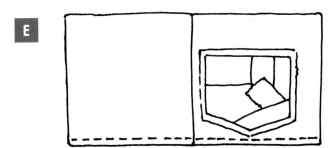

E

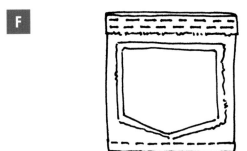

F

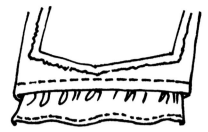

G

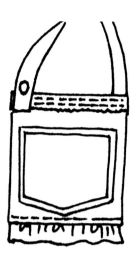

H

10. Baste across the top of ruffle ⅜" below the raw edge. Pull up basting thread until ruffle is the same width as lower edge of bag. Slide top raw edge of ruffle between front and back of jeans leg at hem with right side of fabric on the same side as pocket. Gathered edge should be ½" inside jeans leg. Pin. Stitch across close to lower edge of jeans leg through all thicknesses using thread for use with denim. **SEE FIG. G.**

11. With pocket side of bag facing you, place the button end of your jeans waistband OVER the upper left corner of bag so that lower edge of button is flush with top edge of bag. Pin. Stitch end of waistband to bag. **SEE FIG. H.**

12. Turn bag over and position buttonhole end of waistband on the opposite side of bag so that it overlaps the top left corner. (Make sure not to twist handle.) Pin. Stitch end of waistband to bag.

laptop tote

Just because you're technically savvy doesn't mean you can't indulge your creative impulses. Stand out from the crowd carrying your laptop in this seriously sturdy tote refashioned from denim jeans with a snazzy fabric lining. A vintage tie through the belt loops adds a bohemian element to this functional and chic piece that you can make yourself.

MATERIALS NEEDED

■ Two pair of worn jeans (the sample used men's Levi's, size 34.*)

■ *Optional:* It would be a good idea to have a third pair of jeans for backup.**

■ ½ yard of fabric for the lining

■ Denim needle for machine, seam ripper, thread for use with denim

■ *Optional:* Men's vintage tie

* Larger men's denim jeans work better for this project, because the legs are wider. As a general guide, make sure you can cut a 14" wide piece from the legs when one of the seams is removed and the pant leg is laid out flat.

** Make sure you like the color and/or fading of all the denim jeans you chose when they are all sewn together as a whole. We wanted the purse to look like it was made from one pair of jeans, so we purchase used denim jeans with a similar look. You may like the look of different colors of denim and/or fading to give it a unique look.

A

DISASSEMBLY OF JEANS

1. Determine which one of your jeans you would like to use for the front flap. You will use the right side (front and back).

2. Take the jeans you are using for the front flap and with your seam ripper, rip the outer (single) leg seams up to and in-line with the crotch of both legs. **SEE FIG. A.**

3. Cutting the same jeans, cut the front middle down around the zipper through the crotch and up the back crotch seam through the middle of the waistband. You should now have two separate leg sides of the jeans. Set aside. **SEE FIGS. B & C.**

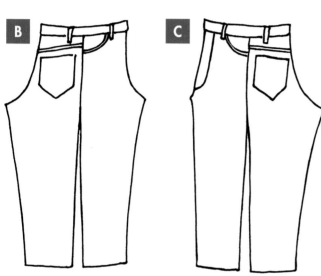

B

C

4. On the second pair of jeans, rip the outer (single) seam of one leg up to the bottom of the back pocket. This leg will be used for your back pocket pattern piece with the hem intact. So make sure you like the look of the hem and it is not too worn or frayed.

5. On the other leg of the second pair of jeans, rip the inner (double) seam up to the crotch.

PATTERN PIECES NEEDED

From Denim Jeans:

Front Flap – 14" wide x 14" high

Front Flap Extension – 14" wide x 6" high

Back of Front Flap – 14" wide x 17" high

Front of Bag – 14" wide x 16½" high

Back of Bag – 14" wide x 16½" high

Back Pocket – 14" wide x 11" high

Sides and Bottom of Bag – 3" wide x 49" long

Strap – Two pieces 3" wide x 47" long

From Lining Fabric:

Front of Lining – 14" wide x 16½" high

Back of Lining – 14" wide x 16½" high

Sides and Bottom of Lining – 3" wide x 49" long

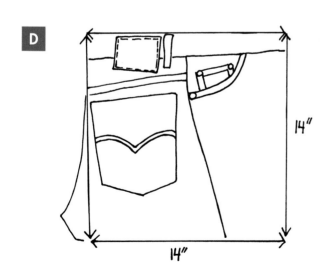

D

14"

14"

CUTTING INSTRUCTIONS FOR TOTE

1. For the front side of the front flap, lay the right leg side of the first pair of jeans on a flat surface. Using the waist band as the top edge of the pattern piece, mark a rectangular pattern piece 14" wide by approximately 14" high. Adjust rectangle as needed to avoid the front zipper, the back double seam, the belt loops, and the brass tacks. Cut it out and set it aside. **SEE FIG. D.**

2. For the front of the tote, unfold and lay this same leg (from Step 1) of the first pair of jeans on a flat surface. With the double seam down the center, measure and cut a rectangular pattern piece 14" wide by 16½" high. Cut this piece close to the bottom edge of the leg. Set jeans aside. **SEE FIG. E.**

3. For the back of the tote, take the second pair of jeans, unfold and lay the leg on a flat surface with the outer single seam intact. With the single seam slightly off center, measure and cut a rectangular pattern piece 14" wide by 16½" high. Cut this piece close to the bottom edge of the leg. **SEE FIG. F.**

4. For the back pocket of the tote, unfold and lay the second leg of the second pair of jeans on a flat surface. With the double seam slightly off center and using the hem of the jeans as the top edge of the back pocket, measure and cut a rectangular pattern piece 14" wide by 11" high. **SEE FIG. G.**

5. For the back side of the front flap, take the second pair of jeans, unfold and lay the leg on a flat surface with the outer single seam intact. Measure and cut a rectangular pattern piece 14" wide by 17" high.

6. For the top extension piece of the front flap, cut a piece from any portion of jeans that is 14" wide by, at a minimum, 6" high.

7. For the tote sides and bottom you will need a strip 3" wide by 49" long. We cut it from the inner (double) seam of the first pair of jeans. You probably will have to piece it together in order to get the length needed. **SEE FIGS. H & I.**

E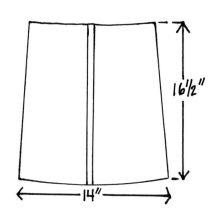

16½"

14"

F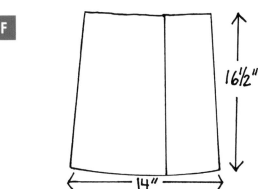

16½"

14"

G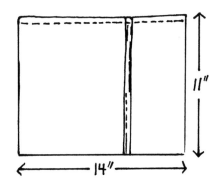

11"

14"

H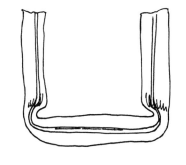

I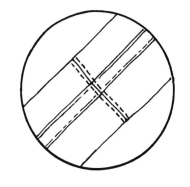

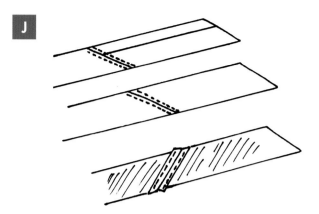

J

8. For the tote strap you will need two strips 3" wide by 47" long. We cut them from various sections of the remaining jean parts and pieced them together. **SEE FIG. J.**

CUTTING INSTRUCTIONS FOR LINING

1. For the front and back of lining cut two pattern pieces from lining fabric 14" wide by 16½" tall.

2. For the lining sides and bottom you will need a strip 3" wide by 49" long. You will have to piece it together in order to get the length needed.

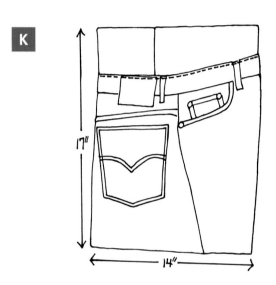

K

17"

14"

ASSEMBLY INSTRUCTIONS FOR TOTE

1. To make the front flap, with both right sides up, lap the top of the waistband of the front flap piece over the bottom raw edge of the front flap extension piece, approximately 1"; pin and top-stitch together close to the finished top edge of the waistband. After the two pieces are sewn together, trim the extension piece so the entire height of the front flap measures 17" high. **SEE FIG. K.**

2. With RST, stitch the front flap piece to the back flap piece. Making sure to leave a 6" opening at the top of the flap piece (the extension end) for turning.

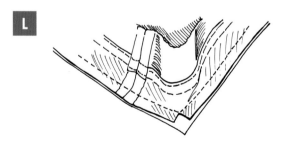

L

3. Trim the corners and turn inside out through the opening and press.

4. Topstitch ¼" from the top and bottom finished edges of the front flap. Set aside.

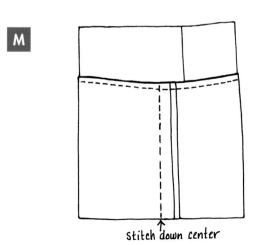

M

stitch down center

5. With RST, place the side/bottom piece on the front tote piece. Starting at the right corner, line up the top and side raw edges. Stitch down the first side using a ½" seam allowance, stopping and backstitching ½" up from bottom raw edge. Clip to the stitch line at the ½" mark on the side/bottom piece. Turn the side/bottom piece, matching it up with the bottom raw edge of the front tote piece. Stitch across the bottom stopping ½" from the left side seam. Again, backstitch and clip to the stitch line on the side/bottom piece. Next, turn the side/bottom piece again, matching it up with the left side raw edge of the front tote piece. Continue to stitch up the left side with a ½" seam allowance. Be sure to backstitch at both bottom corners and at the top of the side seams. Set aside. **SEE FIG. L.**

6. Attach the back pocket to the back tote piece by placing the pocket (right side up) on to the right side of the back bag piece. Align the sides and the bottom raw edges and pin. Baste in place. Topstitch down the center of the pocket, creating two sides to the pocket. Be sure to backstitch at the top of the pocket to reinforce the top edge. **SEE FIG. M.**

7. With RST, attach the back tote piece to the side/bottom piece (which is already attached to the front tote piece) by following Step 5. Clip the corners, press seams open, and turn inside out. Set aside.

8. With RST, stitch the two strap pieces together using a ½" seam down both sides of the strap. Turn right side out and press. Topstitch a ¼" seam down both sides of the strap.

9. With RST, center and place one end of the finished strap on the outside of the side piece, aligning the top raw edges, and stitch within the ½" seam allowance. Repeat for the opposite end of the finished strap, making sure not to twist the strap in the process.

10. Press a ½" hem to the wrong side of the fabric around the entire top raw edge of the denim tote. Once you fold the top raw edge of both the side sections to the inside, the strap is now in its upright position.

ASSEMBLY INSTRUCTIONS FOR LINING

1. Follow Step 5 for sewing the lining together, attaching the front and back lining pieces to the side/bottom lining piece. Clip corners and press seams open.

2. Press a ½" hem to the wrong side of the fabric around the entire top raw edge of the lining.

3. With WST, place the lining inside the denim tote, lining up the top folded edges and the side seams. Topstitch the top of the tote closed close to the two folded edges, catching the ends of the strap in the stitching.

FINAL ASSEMBLY INSTRUCTIONS

1. To attach the front flap to the back side of the tote, with both right sides up, lap the top edge of the flap over the top edge of the back by approximately 1" and pin. Topstitch together close to the finished top edge of the flap piece and at the finished top edge of the back of the tote. These two stitch lines will be approximately 1" apart. Be sure to backstitch at the sides of the flap to reinforce.

2. Optional: Weave a man's vintage tie through the belt loops on the front flap of the tote. Trim ends so that they wrap around the edges of the flap and hand stitch in place.

denim quest quilt

MATERIALS NEEDED

- Several pairs of children's denim jeans (enough to cut (48) 6½" squares)

- 3 yards of fabric for backing and binding (we used Moda's 54" cotton velvet)

- One crib-size cotton batting

- Thread to match denim

- Thread to match backing and binding fabric

- Denim needle for machine and thread for use with denim

- Plastic straight edge template

- Large rotary cutter

- Curved basting pins

- *Optional:* 6½" square plastic template

The shades, weights, and textures of each square in this quilt vary as your eye travels across its landscape. With its cotton velvet backing and substantial feel, it lends itself well to snuggling up with a favorite book or movie. As a decorative piece, its variety of colors and textural elements and with a few needle worked pieces thrown in, construct a handcrafted, contemporary quilt created of memories. The finished size is 40" wide by 52" long.

CUTTING INSTRUCTIONS

1. Using the 6½" square plastic template, start cutting out quilt squares from various locations on the children's jeans. Be creative when cutting the quilt squares; refer to the picture of the quilt sample shown. We cut about half of the squares from plain, solid sections of the jeans and the other half from locations on the jeans that would include pockets, sections with seams, loops, patches, etc. An assortment of blocks makes the quilt more interesting.

2. Cut a total of 48 denim quilt squares.

ASSEMBLY INSTRUCTIONS

1. On a large flat surface lay out the quilt squares, six across and eight down. Alternate the various colors and patterns of the denim squares until you like the look.

2. Once you are satisfied with your pattern, start stitching the squares together. With RST and using a ¼" seam allowance, start sewing the six across together. Repeat for each row of six until all eight rows are complete. After each row is complete, place it back on the flat surface in its original order.

3. With RST, take row one and place it on row two, lining up at the seams, pin and stitch together using a ¼" seam allowance.

4. Next, place row two on top of row three, lining up at the seams, pin, and stitch until all eight rows are sewn together to form one complete quilt top. Set aside.

5. On a large flat surface unfold and lay out the crib batting. With the right side up, center and lay the completed denim quilt top over the cotton batting. Baste the two layers together. We used curved basting pins to baste the two layers together.

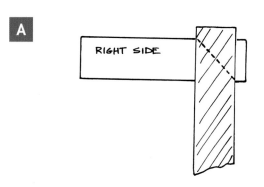

A

RIGHT SIDE

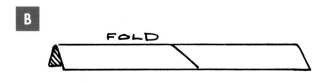

B

FOLD

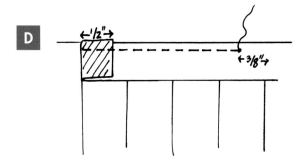

C

QUILT CENTER

FOLD OF BINDING

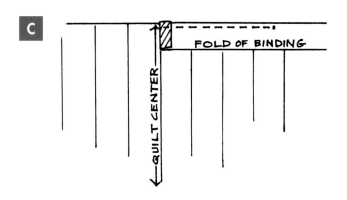

D

←1/2"→

←3/8"→

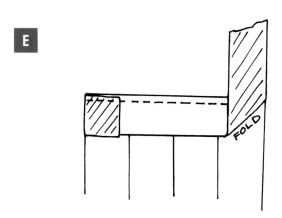

E

FOLD

6. Using the denim colored sewing thread, machine quilt the denim quilt/batting top, using the stitch-in-the-ditch method. Stitch both the vertical and the horizontal seams of the quilt top. Set aside.

7. Again, on a large flat surface lay out the fabric backing with the wrong side up, center and lay the quilted denim quilt top on top of the backing. Following the denim quilt top's raw edge, machine baste all three layers together at all four sides. After the three layers are machine basted together, trim the excess batting and backing fabric flush with the raw edge of the denim quilt top. Set aside.

8. To make the binding, cut several 8" wide strips on the straight grain of the remaining backing fabric. Cut enough strips to attach around the perimeter raw edge of the denim lap quilt.

9. Join the 8" wide strips with diagonal seams to make one continuous binding strip. Trim the excess fabric, leaving ½" seam allowances. Press the seam allowances open. Then, with the wrong sides together, fold the binding strip in half lengthwise and press. **SEE FIGS. A & B.**

10. Beginning in the center of one side, place the binding strip against the right side of the quilt top, aligning the binding strip's raw edges with the quilt top's raw edge. Fold over the beginning of the binding strip about ½". Stitch using a ⅜" seam allowance, through all layers, stopping ⅜" from the corner. Backstitch, and then clip the threads. Remove the quilt from under the sewing machine presser foot. **SEE FIGS. C & D.**

11. Fold the binding strip upward, creating a diagonal fold, and finger-press. **SEE FIG. E.**

12. Holding the diagonal fold in place with your finger, bring the binding strip down in line with the next edge, making a horizontal fold that aligns with the top edge of the quilt. Start sewing again at the top of the horizontal fold, stitching through all layers. Sew around the quilt, turning each corner in the same manner. When you return to the starting point, lap the binding strip end over the beginning fold. **SEE FIG. F.**

13. Turn the binding over the edge to the back of the quilt. This will create a binding strip approximately 1¾" wide. Hand-stitch the binding to the backing fabric, making sure to cover any machine stitching. To make mitered corners on the back, hand-stitch the binding up to a corner; fold a miter in the binding. Take a stitch or two in the fold to secure it. Then stitch the binding in place up to the next corner. Finish each corner in the same manner.

F

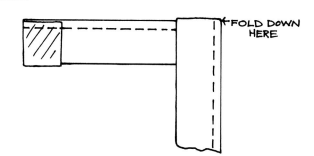

FOLD DOWN HERE

resources

Supplies you need for making these projects are sold at your local craft and quilt shops.

Most of the supplies are also available on our websites:

indygojunction.com
thevintageworkshop.com

or call (913) 341-5559

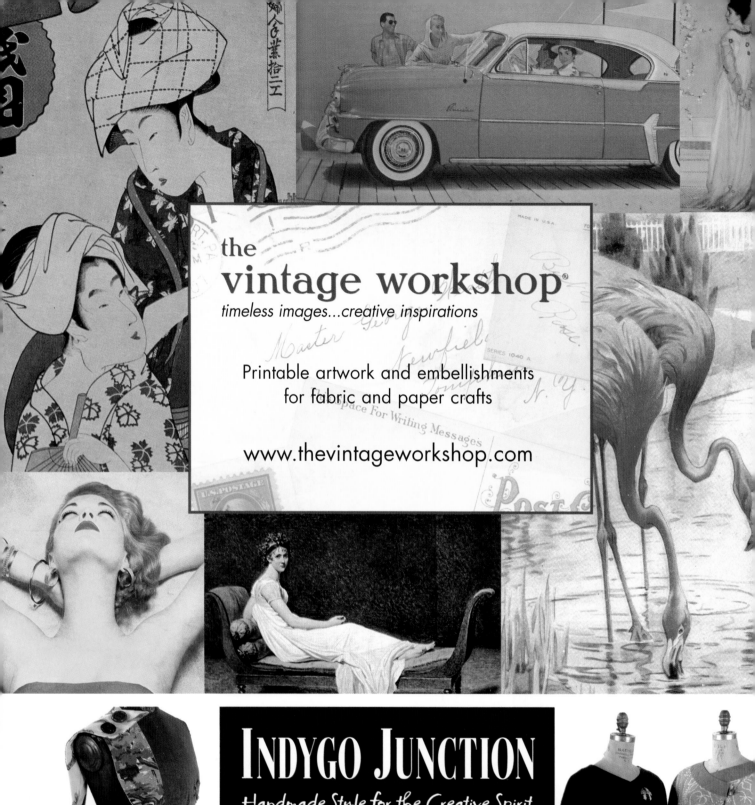